最新時事テーマ収録
Readings at the **EXAM REQUIRED** level

Cutting Edge

ナビブック 付

速読トレーニング
文構造解説
重要語句

Green

本書は、大学入試レベルへの英文読解力を段階的に養成できるように編集されています。

英文素材について	① 新しい素材で、「読む価値がある英文」であること ② 文系・理系のテーマのバランスを取ること ③ 難易度にバラつきがでないこと を基準に厳選しました。そうして選ばれた英文を、段階的に入試レベルの読解力を養成できるように配列しています。
設問について	「構文・語彙」など入試の設問になりやすい部分と、内容理解のポイントとなる部分に、英文の流れに沿って設問を配置しています。設問をはじめから解いていくことで、内容が理解できる構成になっています。
「Navi Book」について	英文学習をより深く、より効率的なものにするためにも付属「Navi Book」の活用をおすすめいたします。「Navi Book」では、英文内の重要語句をレベル別にほぼ全て網羅しており、覚えるべき語句とそうでないものが一目瞭然になっています。また「英単語」→「日本語の意味」の順で読み上げた音声もあるので、より効果的な単語学習ができるようになっています。英文中の分かりづらい構文や複雑な文構造についても解説していますので、問題を解いた後でしっかりと確認し、分からなかった部分を次に残さないようにしましょう。加えて、英文要約に段階的に取り組める問題も用意しています。
用語解説について	本文で触れられている用語の解説を巻末にまとめています。英文で取り上げられる歴史や社会問題、人物名などに関する背景知識があれば、英文の理解度も増すことでしょう。問題に取り組む際には、是非この解説も活用してください。

【本書の説明】

★ 英文素材は全て入試で出題されたもので、変更はしていません。（一部、英文校閲による入試問題の明らかな誤りや誤植があった場合のみ、修正を加えています）

★ 語注はすべて実際の入試問題で明記されているものです。

★ 右端に大学名がある設問は、出題校で実際に出題された問題です。その他の設問は、出題傾向、難易度、記述・客観のバランスに合わせて作成されたオリジナル問題です。

Contents

1.

テーマ	環境
語 数	359 words
出題校	近畿大

Recently, researchers from the Union of Concerned Scientists in the U.S. ◑1-1 released a report on how consumer behavior affects the environment. Their study showed that meat consumption is one of the main ways that humans can damage the environment, second only to the use of motor vehicles.

⁵ So, how can a simple thing like eating meat have a negative effect on the ◑1-2 environment? The most important impact of meat production is through the use of water and land. Two thousand five hundred gallons of water are needed to produce one pound of beef, whereas only twenty gallons of water are needed to produce one pound of wheat.

¹⁰ (1)By producing crops instead of animals, we can make more efficient use of the ◑1-3 land and water. One acre of farmland that is used for raising livestock can produce 250 pounds of beef. One acre of farmland used for crops can produce 40,000 pounds of potatoes, 30,000 pounds of carrots, or 50,000 pounds of tomatoes.

Furthermore, (2)farm animals add to the problem of global warming. All ◑1-4 ¹⁵ livestock animals such as cows, pigs, and sheep release methane★ by expelling gas from their bodies. One cow can produce up to sixty liters of methane each day. Methane gas is the second most common greenhouse gas after carbon dioxide. Many environmental experts now believe that methane is more responsible for global warming than carbon dioxide. It is estimated that twenty-five percent of all methane ²⁰ released into the atmosphere comes from farm animals.

People are becoming aware of the benefits of switching to a vegetarian diet, not ◑1-5 just for health reasons, but also because it plays a vital role in protecting the environment. (3)Some people go further, and eat a vegan diet, which excludes all products from animal sources, such as cheese, eggs, and milk. However, some ²⁵ nutritionists believe that a vegan diet can be deficient in some of the vitamins and minerals that our bodies need daily.

Today, many people are concerned about improving their health, and about ◑1-6 protecting the environment. Switching to a vegetarian diet — or just eating less meat — is a good way to do both of these things at the same time.

★ methane「メタンガス」

1 第 2 段落の内容と一致するものを 1 つ選びなさい。 (近畿大)

① Eating beef has a harmful effect on water usage but not on land usage.

② Far less water is used in the production of wheat than in the production of meat.

③ Producing meat requires much water, but the amount of water needed is unknown.

④ The amount of water used in producing beef does not have a negative effect on the environment.

2 下線部（1）を和訳しなさい。

_____

_____

3 下線部（2）について、その理由は何か、日本語で答えなさい。

_____

_____

4 下線部（3）について、その具体的な内容を本文に即して日本語で説明しなさい。

_____

_____

5 本文の内容と一致するものを 2 つ選びなさい。 (近畿大・改)

① The human consumption of meat is the second most damaging behavior on the environment.

② Altogether, 120,000 pounds of vegetables can be produced from one acre of land.

③ A greater amount of methane produced by livestock has led to decreased crop production.

④ Farm animals are responsible for nearly all of the methane released into the atmosphere.

⑤ A vegan diet is not just healthier, but is also better for the environment than a vegetable diet.

⑥ Not eating as much meat both protects the environment and improves people's health.

2.

テーマ	健康
語　数	426 words
出題校	名城大

How much water do you think an ordinary person really needs to drink per day? 🔊1-11 Many people believe they are supposed to drink eight glasses of water a day, or about two liters. Why? Because that is what they have been told all their lives. But a recent report offers some different advice. Experts say people should obey their bodies; they should drink as much water as they feel like drinking.

The report says most healthy people meet their daily needs for liquid by (1)letting 🔊1-12 thirst be their guide. The report is from the Institute of Medicine, part of the American National Academies. This organization provides scientific and technical advice to the government and the public. The report contains some general suggestions. The experts say women should get about 2.7 liters of water daily. Men should get about 3.7 liters. But wait — in each case, those are more than eight glasses. There is one important difference. The report does not tell people how many glasses of water to drink. In fact, the experts say it may be impossible to know how many glasses are needed to meet these guidelines. This is because the daily water requirement can include the water content in foods.

(2)People do not get water only by forcing themselves to drink a set number of 🔊1-13 glasses of it per day. People also drink fruit juices and sodas or milk. Of course they may also drink coffee and tea. These all contain water. Yet some also contain caffeine. This causes the body to get rid of more water. But the writers of the report say this does not mean the body loses too much water. As you might expect, the Institute of Medicine says people usually need to drink more water when they are physically active. (3)The same is true of those who live in hot climates. Depending on heat and activity, some people could drink two times as much water as others do.

All this, however, does not answer one question. No one seems sure why people 🔊1-14 have the idea that good health requires eight glasses of water daily. It may have started with (4)a misunderstanding. In 1945, the American National Academy of Sciences published (5)some guidelines. Its Food and Nutrition Board* said a good amount of water for most adults was 2.5 liters daily. This was based on an average of one milliliter for each kilocalorie of food eaten. But that was only part of what the board said. It also said that most of this amount is contained in prepared foods.

* Food and Nutrition Board「食品栄養部会」

1 下線部（1）の letting thirst be their guide を言いかえたものとして最も適切なものを、1つ選びなさい。

① asking advice from people who have recovered from thirst
② drinking as much water as their doctors advise them to do
③ judging from their natural feeling of how thirsty they are
④ drinking as much as possible while having a meal

2 下線部（2）を和訳しなさい。

_____

_____

3 下線部（3）の The same とは何を指しているか、日本語で答えなさい。

_____

4 下線部（4）の a misunderstanding の具体的な内容をまとめた記述にするために、2つの空所にそれぞれ 15 字以内の日本語を書きなさい。

公表された 1 日に必要な水分量の大半は ⬚⬚⬚⬚⬚⬚⬚⬚⬚⬚⬚⬚⬚⬚⬚
⬚⬚⬚⬚⬚ いたが、その水分量を ⬚⬚⬚⬚⬚⬚⬚⬚⬚⬚⬚⬚⬚⬚⬚
⬚⬚⬚⬚⬚ だと誤解したこと。

5 下線部（5）の some guidelines によれば、アメリカの成人が 1 日あたり 2,500 キロカロリーの食物を摂取した場合、通常どれくらいの量の水をとる必要があると推定されるか。次の（　）の中に入る適切な数字を答えなさい。

（　　　　　）liters

6 本文の内容と一致するものを 1 つ選びなさい。

① More and more people think that drinking eight glasses of water a day is too much to be good for their health.
② The experts in the report insisted that people need to drink more water than many people seem to understand.
③ The recent report implies the amount of water we should drink depends on the water amount in the food we eat.
④ It is beneficial for people to get a certain amount of caffeine, especially for people who drink few liquids.

3.

テーマ	言語
語　数	442 words
出題校	宮城教育大

One interesting thing about languages is the way they change over time. In ⊙1-19 English, everything from spelling to vocabulary to pronunciation has gone through major changes over centuries. (1)In fact, to a modern speaker, the English of 1,000 years ago is like a foreign language!

5　The history of English dates back around 1,500 years. At that time, groups of ⊙1-20 Europeans invaded England, bringing their languages with them. These gradually developed into Old English. Later, in 1066, England was invaded by the Normans, from France. This caused the language to go through an important shift, leading to what we now call Middle English. Over the next 500 years, the language underwent 10 further shifts, eventually evolving into Modern English. As the language has developed down to the present day, many things about it have changed.

Pronunciation is one of the most obvious areas of change. For example, in Old ⊙1-21 English, people said "hus" and "mus." Now we say "house" and "mouse." These days, there are also many differences in the way English is pronounced in the USA, 15　the UK, Australia, and elsewhere. (2)When people who speak the same language live in places separated by great distances, the language undergoes rapid changes in each place.

Spelling has also gone through interesting changes. For example, in Old English, ⊙1-22 people wrote "riht." A "g" was added in Middle English, making the spelling "right." 20　Also, in the distant past, people did not always follow standards of spelling. In the 18th and 19th centuries, scholars like Noah Webster wrote dictionaries which made English spelling more consistent. But different standards were decided on in England and the USA, so some differences remain — for example, "color" vs. "colour."

(3)Vocabulary changes happen even more quickly. English has grown by ⊙1-23 25　borrowing words from languages such as French, Spanish, and Arabic, to name a few. This often happens with food. "Tofu" and "sushi" are now standard English words, for example, and even "edamame" is listed in some dictionaries. (4)Then there is slang, with new terms entering and leaving the language every year. Thirty years ago, you often heard people saying "groovy," meaning "great." These days, you 30　rarely hear the word, except in old movies and on old TV shows.

Because English is spoken by so many people worldwide, it really is (5)an exciting ⊙1-24 time for the language. Just as American and British versions are always changing, so are versions spoken in Canada, Singapore, India, and elsewhere. At the same time, an entire new version of English is appearing on the Internet, with whole new slang expressions and writing styles. So in a way, learning English is a never-ending process, even for native speakers!

1 下線部 (1) のように言える理由を日本語で答えなさい。

_____

2 下線部 (2) を和訳しなさい。 （宮城教育大）

_____

_____

3 下線部 (3) のようになる理由を日本語で説明しなさい。

_____

_____

4 下線部 (4) を和訳しなさい。 （宮城教育大）

_____

_____

5 下線部 (5) で an exciting time と著者が述べている理由を 1 つ選びなさい。

① English is spoken all over the world and that has made it easier than ever to communicate with people living in various places.

② English has gone through so many changes that even native speakers find it hard to understand new versions of English.

③ Different places in the world where English is spoken have produced new styles of English, which makes learning English even more interesting.

④ Throughout the world, English has a lot of new versions and sometimes that can confuse even native speakers.

6 本文の内容に合うものを 1 つ選びなさい。

① The invasion of England by the Normans in the 11th century helped to create so-called Modern English.

② English has changed a lot in pronunciation, but that is not so obvious as in the area of spelling.

③ In spite of the efforts of scholars who aimed at the uniformity of English spelling, there are some differences left between British English and American English.

④ The most important factor in creating new versions of English is the new terms and expressions found on the Internet.

4.

テーマ	科学
語　数	327 words
出題校	東洋大

　　Some rich people are planning to upload their brains onto computers after they　🔊1-29
die, hoping that science will progress enough to make artificial intelligence possible.
If you think this sounds like science fiction, take a look at the work of Martine
Rothblatt, America's highest paid female CEO★ and founder of GeoStar, a GPS★
5　navigation company. Rothblatt also started Sirius Satellite Radio, a service allowing
customers to hear nearly a thousand different radio stations online. In 2007 she
created a simple copy of her partner's brain and uploaded it into a life-like robot
known as (1)Bina48. That robot is able to have short ordinary conversations with
humans. However, Bina48 is not yet able to sustain long conversations in ways that
10　seem fully "human."

　　Rothblatt believes that within twenty years, "mind clones★" will be humanity's　🔊1-30
biggest invention. (2)The concept of cloning human brains and placing them inside
robotic bodies has been described in numerous science fiction works. However,
Google director Ray Kurzweil believes that our bodies may be replaced by machines
15　within ninety years and that some people will become digitally immortal★. His 1999
book *The Age of Spiritual Machines: When Computers Exceed Human Intelligence*
describes one possible future in which the boundaries between biological human
intelligence and digital artificial intelligence blur★. Kurzweil mentions a possible
future that seems both (3)promising and terrifying. If super intelligent transhumans★
20　become hundreds of times smarter, many problems such as hunger, war, and pollution
could be solved. However, (4)there is no guarantee that such computer-based
intelligence would act "fairly" by ordinary human standards. According to Kurzweil,
during the late 21st century humans who become part of super-intelligent AI systems★
might start to regard ordinary humans as second-class citizens. At some point,
25　ordinary people simply will not be able to keep up with the super-intelligent
"transhumans." If you had the choice and could afford it, would you upload your
own consciousness onto a computer? Would you like to purchase a robotic version
of yourself?

　　★　CEO「最高経営責任者」　GPS「全地球測位システム」　clone「クローン」
　　immortal「不死身の」　blur「あいまいになる」　transhuman「トランスヒューマン、超人間」
　　AI system「人工知能システム」

1 下線部（1）の Bina48 の特徴を日本語で簡潔に説明しなさい。

_____

_____

2 下線部（2）を和訳しなさい。

_____

_____

3 下線部（3）の promising について、その具体的な内容を日本語で答えなさい。

_____

_____

4 下線部（4）を和訳しなさい。

_____

_____

5 次の（1）、（2）に対する答えとして最も適切なものを、それぞれ1つずつ選びなさい。 （東洋大）

(1) **Which statement is true about Martine Rothblatt?**

① She is Ray Kurzweil's boss.

② She is a rich executive.

③ She hired a robot named Bina48.

④ Her partner wants to clone her.

(2) **What concern is expressed if Ray Kurzweil's forecast about "spiritual machines" becomes true?**

① Current humans might not be able to solve many of the world's problems.

② It might not be possible to "upload" brains onto computer systems.

③ It will probably be too costly for all persons to become transhumans.

④ The gap between ordinary humans and new "transhumans" might create conflicts.

5.

テ ー マ	動物
語 数	378 words
出題校	武蔵大

Have you ever heard of the "quagga"? Perhaps not, but you may have seen a zebra before. The zebra is a horse-like animal with distinctive black and white stripes covering its body. The quagga was a member of the zebra family, brownish in colour with white stripes around the neck and the front part of the body. It is often said that quaggas looked like "(1)zebras which had forgotten to put on their pajama trousers." Quaggas lived in Southern Africa, but they died out in the 19th century due to overhunting. We can now only see their wild beauty as stuffed specimens.

Some researchers, however, have tried to "revive" the quagga. (2)Because of its attractive stripe pattern, the quagga has gathered much attention from those interested in animal conservation. Those who would like to see the animals walk around the savannas again have conducted the Quagga Project for over thirty years in South Africa. It turns out that the quagga is genetically close to the plains zebra★. In this project, researchers have attempted to selectively breed plains zebras: they chose plains zebras which have fewer stripes and look slightly like quaggas. Baby zebras born to a slightly quagga-like mother and father may look more like the quagga, with a significantly reduced number of stripes. This project has achieved a certain level of success, producing several lovely baby zebras which have striking similarities to the quagga.

However, should we be happy about this? While this new generation of zebras is visually impressive, it only resembles the quagga in appearance. The fact is that these zebras are genetically different from quaggas. (3)The more we look at these young, cute, quagga-like zebras, the more we are forced to face the sad truth that the quagga died out because of our abuse of nature. Does this project help restore nature to its original state? Or is it just for the self-satisfaction of guilt-ridden human beings?

Furthermore, it is notable that people are interested in quaggas because they are beautiful in appearance. (4)It is said that good-looking endangered★ animals tend to attract attention and money from people, but that plain-looking endangered animals are often ignored. This suggests that human beings are biased towards beauty and ugliness even when it comes to environmental causes.

★ plains zebra「サバンナシマウマ」　endangered「絶滅の危険にさらされている」

1 下線部（1）について、quagga はどんな外見をしていたか、本文に即して日本語で説明しなさい。

_____

_____

2 下線部（2）を和訳しなさい。（quagga は「クアッガ」とする。）

_____

_____

_____

3 第2段落の内容と一致するものを1つ選びなさい。 （武蔵大）

① In the Quagga Project, baby zebras born to a slightly quagga-like mother and father had more stripes than their parents.

② In the Quagga Project, quagga-like animals have been bred by researchers from plains zebras with fewer stripes.

③ The Quagga Project failed in producing many baby zebras that resembled the quagga.

④ The Quagga Project was conducted by those with little interest in animal conservation in South Africa.

4 下線部（3）を和訳しなさい。

_____

_____

_____

5 下線部（4）について、このことからどういったことが言えると筆者は述べているか、日本語で答えなさい。

_____

_____

_____

6 本文の内容に一致するものを1つ選びなさい。 （武蔵大・改）

① Some researchers have tried to "revive" the quagga in the Quagga Project, which lasted for only a few years in South Africa.

② The abuse of nature by human beings caused the disappearance of quaggas.

③ The quagga is a member of the zebra family and still lives in South Africa.

④ Those who are interested in plain-looking endangered animals do not like quagga-like zebras.

6.

テーマ	エッセイ
語数	355 words
出題校	関西学院大

The host poured tea into the cup and placed it on the small table in front of his ⊙ 1-43 guests, who were a father and a daughter, and put the lid on the cup with a light sound. Apparently thinking of something, he hurried into the inner room, leaving the thermos★ on the table. His two guests heard a chest of drawers opening and a rustling.

5　They remained sitting in the parlor★, the ten-year-old daughter looking at the flowers outside the window, the father just about to take his cup, when the crash came, right there in the parlor. Something was irreparably broken.

It was the thermos, which had fallen to the floor. The girl looked over her shoulder abruptly, startled, staring. (1)It was mysterious. Neither of them had touched it, not 10　even a little bit. True, it hadn't stood steadily when their host placed it on the table, but it hadn't fallen then.

(2)The crash of the thermos caused the host, with a box of sugar cubes in his hand, ⊙ 1-44 to rush back from the inner room. He looked at the steaming floor and cried out, "It doesn't matter! It doesn't matter!"

15　The father started to say something. Then he muttered, "Sorry, I touched it and it fell."

"It doesn't matter," the host said.

Later, when they left the house, the daughter said, "Daddy, did you touch it?"

"No. But it stood so close to me."

20　"But you didn't touch it. I saw your reflection in the mirror. You were sitting perfectly still.

The father laughed. "What then would you give as the cause of its fall?"

"The thermos fell by itself. The floor is uneven. It wasn't steady when Mr. Li put it there. (3)Daddy, why did you say that you ..."

25　"(4)That won't do, girl. It sounds more acceptable when I say I knocked it down. ⊙ 1-45 There are things which people accept less the more you defend them. (5)The truer the story you tell is, the less true it sounds."

The daughter was lost in silence for a while. Then she said, "Can you explain it only this way?"

30　"Only this way," her father said.

★ thermos「魔法びん」 parlor「客間」

1 下線部（1）でなぜ mysterious と言っているのか、その理由を日本語で答えなさい。

_____

_____

2 下線部（2）を和訳しなさい。

_____

_____

3 下線部（3）の … に省略されているのはどのような言葉だと考えられるか、日本語で答えなさい。

_____

_____

4 下線部（4）（5）の意味として最も適切なものを、それぞれ1つずつ選びなさい。 （関西学院大）

(4) **That won't do**

① That will be defending   ② That will be losing

③ That will not be acceptable   ④ That will not be true

(5) **The truer the story you tell is, the less true it sounds.**

① Even though you tell an untrue story, it sounds true.

② Only when you tell a true story, it sounds true.

③ The true story you tell turns out to be less false.

④ When you tell a true story, it sounds less true.

5 本文の内容と一致するものを2つ選びなさい。

① The thermos fell to the floor when the father and the little daughter were talking with the host in the parlor.

② The daughter saw the father touch the thermos, causing it to fall to the floor.

③ When the host knew that the thermos was completely broken, he got very angry with the father.

④ Although he was not actually responsible for the crash of the thermos, the father told the host that he was.

⑤ The father thought that lying is sometimes the best thing to do in order to avoid troubles.

⑥ The daughter was satisfied with the father's explanation for what he had done.

7.

テーマ	進化論
語　数	359 words
出題校	甲南大

It is often thought that when humans first learned how to control fire, one of its ⊙1-50 major effects was to keep people warm, but (1)that idea wrongly implies that our pre-cooking ancestors would have had difficulty staying warm without fire. Chimpanzees survive nights exposed to long, cold rain-storms. Gorillas sleep uncovered in high, cool mountains. Every species other than humans can maintain body heat without fire. (2)When our ancestors first controlled fire, they would not have needed it for warmth, (A) fire would have saved them some energy in maintaining body temperature.

But the opportunity to be warmed by fire created new options. Humans are ⊙1-51 exceptional runners, far better than chimpanzees and gorillas, and perhaps better even than wolves and horses, at running long distances. The problem for most animals is that they easily become overheated when they run. A chimpanzee sits exhausted after only five minutes' hard exercise, breathing heavily and visibly hot, with sweat pouring out of its body. Most animals cannot develop a solution to this problem because they need something to maintain body heat during rest or sleep, such as a thick coat of hair. (3)This, of course, cannot be removed after exercise.

The best way to lose heat is not to have a lot of body hair in the first place. A ⊙1-52 scientist, Peter Wheeler, has long argued that (4)this may be why humans are "naked apes": a reduction in hair might have allowed them to avoid becoming overheated on the hot savanna. But early humans could have lost their hair only if they had had an alternative system for maintaining body heat at night. Fire offers such a system. Once our ancestors controlled fire, they were able to keep warm even when they were resting. The benefit must have been high: the loss of their hair probably made humans better able to travel long distances during hot periods, when most animals are (B). They could then run for long distances when hunting animals. By allowing body hair to be lost, the control of fire increased humans' ability to run long distances making them better able to hunt or steal meat from rival species.

1 下線部（1）の that idea の内容を日本語で説明しなさい。

_____

_____

2 下線部（2）を和訳しなさい。

_____

_____

3 下線部（3）を This が指すものを明らかにして和訳しなさい。

_____

_____

4 下線部（4）の this の内容を日本語で説明しなさい。

_____

_____

5 空所（A）（B）に入る適切な語を、それぞれ1つずつ選びなさい。 （甲南大）

(A)

① as far as ② because ③ so that ④ although

(B)

① hunting ② inactive ③ naked ④ feeding

6 次の文の中から、本文の内容に一致するものを3つ選びなさい。 （甲南大）

① One might think that humans had had no means of keeping themselves warm before they learned how to control fire, but this is not true.

② Humans are the only species that can keep their body temperature high enough to survive without fire.

③ Only five minutes' hard exercise is enough to make a chimpanzee exhausted and sweat a lot.

④ Losing body hair enabled humans to run even faster.

⑤ When early humans lost their body hair, they tried to find another way to keep warm, and so learned to use fire.

⑥ Thanks to a reduction in body hair, humans became better at traveling long distances and therefore more successful at hunting.

8.

テーマ	社会
語　数	484 words
出題校	フェリス女学院大

Hita Gupta was heartbroken upon learning that her regular visits to nursing homes 🔊 1-56 were put on hold because of the coronavirus.

"They told me that I couldn't visit because they were trying to limit interaction with seniors to prevent the spread of the virus," Hita told CNN.

The 15-year-old had been volunteering at one facility near her home in Paoli, Pennsylvania, for more than a year — organizing activities like trivia quizzes and bingo for the residents.

"The seniors aren't able to see their families, so that's causing loneliness, boredom and anxiety," she said.

And then she thought of her own grandparents.

"They're in India but I have calls with them on Skype★. Even though they have to stay home, we can speak to them. The nursing home residents may not have that option," Hita explained.

So, she came up with the idea to send goodie bags★ — each one filled with one 🔊 1-57 large-print puzzle book, an adult coloring book, and coloring pencils.

"The puzzle and coloring books will help nursing home residents stimulate their minds and keep them occupied," said Hita.

The packages also include an encouraging note written by her 9-year-old brother, Divit. "My brother helps me a lot. It's a lot of work."

Hita coordinates with the nursing homes ahead of time to confirm that the bags can be received safely.

"I call them and say I'm going to leave the boxes outside the front door. They usually leave them out for a few days to make sure there aren't any germs★ before passing them out to the residents."

She has now sent packages to 23 nursing homes in the Philadelphia area.

"Cheering them up makes me happy. Even if it's just for one day."

Initially, Hita was purchasing items with her own pocket money, but figured if she 🔊 1-58 wanted to make a larger impact, she would need more money.

As news spread of her good deed, more people wanted to help.

"I've heard from a lot of people and people are sharing on social media. They've reached out saying, 'You've inspired me to do a similar project in my area.'"

The second-year high school student has created a GoFundMe★ account to help make even more of the thoughtful packages.

"(1)It makes me feel happy that she is able to give back to the community. She's able to let them know that they're not alone and there's a community that stands with them. I am very proud," Hita's mom, Swati, said.

The teenager says she will continue doing this until the public health crisis is over.

"Loneliness is now a bigger problem than ever with our social distancing guidelines. (2)We need to let nursing home residents know that they are not being forgotten, and that they are not alone. As a community, we need to work together to make seniors feel loved and valued."

> * Skype「インターネット通話サービス」 goodie bag「（品物などの）詰め合わせ」
> germ「病原菌」 GoFundMe「募金をするために用いるインターネット・サービス」

1 What is happening because older people living in seniors' homes can't see their families? Answer in Japanese.

_____

_____

2 Translate the underlined sentence (1) into Japanese.

_____

3 Translate the underlined sentence (2) into Japanese.

_____

_____

4 Choose one statement that is true according to the passage. （フェリス女学院大・改）
① The coronavirus prevented Hita from visiting the nursery near her house.
② Hita could hardly stay in touch with her grandparents, who lived in India.
③ Hita thought that the seniors in the nursing homes would be cheered up by her presents such as puzzles and coloring books.
④ Initially, the nursing homes refused Hita's offer because they feared the spread of the virus.

5 Choose one statement that is true according to the passage. （フェリス女学院大・改）
① Hita's presents reached more than twenty nursing homes located in the Philadelphia area.
② People who learned about Hita's activity invited her to their community.
③ In order to expand her activity, Hita donated her pocket money to the funds for the elderly.
④ Hita has the intention to continue her activity as long as the nursing homes ask her to.

9.

テーマ	経済
語数	468 words
出題校	日本大

The current minimum wage in the United States is $7.25 per hour. That means ⊘1-63 that a person working full time (40 hours per week) earns $290 per week, or $15,080 per year. In most parts of the country, this is not enough to pay for basic necessities. In Philadelphia, for example, the average rent for a one-bedroom apartment is more than $1,600 per month. A person working full time at minimum wage in Philadelphia simply cannot afford to live there. I believe that the minimum wage should be replaced by a 'living wage' which would provide a full-time worker with enough income to live on.

We haven't always had (1)this problem. In the early 1970s, even the lowest-paid ⊘1-64 employees earned enough money to provide for themselves, and (2)far fewer families required two incomes in order to live comfortably. Even though workers are more productive today, wages have remained about the same. In the meantime, the cost of necessities (such as housing, health care, child care, education, and transportation) has increased greatly. In short, wages have not kept up with the cost of living.

Those in favor of a living wage, which would vary depending on the cost of living ⊘1-65 in a particular city, believe that earning a living wage should be guaranteed as a human right. Everyone has the right to be paid fairly for their labor, they say. They also claim two economic benefits of a living wage. First, a living wage would reduce the number of people receiving money from the government to buy necessities. This reduces the financial burden on taxpayers. Second, if people have more money, they are likely to spend it in their local communities, buying the items they need from local businesses. (3)This, supporters suggest, will increase profits, create jobs, and strengthen local economies.

Those against a living wage argue that the economic effects on local businesses ⊘1-66 and economies could be very negative. (4)They point to the burden placed on small businesses. If a fast food restaurant, for example, is required to raise the hourly wage of all of its employees by as much as 40%, the owners will be forced to raise prices to cover their increased costs. Some companies may be forced to cut jobs, while others may have to close completely because they can no longer remain competitive and make a profit. Under these conditions, local economies are likely to suffer as prices increase and employment decreases.

Some cities have already passed living wage laws, which require local employers ⊘1-67 to pay employees at a rate that is much higher than the minimum wage. However, these laws have only recently been put into action, and it is too soon to judge their

effectiveness. More data are needed in order to determine if these laws improve the 35
lives of working people.

1 次の質問に対する答えとして、適切なものを 1 つ選びなさい。 （日本大）

Why does the author refer to the cost of an apartment in Philadelphia?

① To encourage people to live outside of the city.

② To encourage people to work more if they want to live in Philadelphia.

③ To show that people earning the minimum wage cannot afford to live there.

④ To show that Philadelphia is the most expensive city to live in.

2 下線部（1）の this problem が生まれた原因は何か、日本語で簡潔に答えなさい。

_____

_____

3 下線部（2）を和訳しなさい。

_____

_____

4 下線部（3）は何を指しているか、適切なものを 1 つ選びなさい。 （日本大）

① Government reducing the financial burden on taxpayers.

② People spending their increased wages locally.

③ Fewer people relying on assistance from the government.

④ Viewing a living wage as a human right.

5 下線部（4）を、They が指すものを明らかにして和訳しなさい。

_____

_____

6 次の質問に対する答えとして、最も適切なものを 1 つ選びなさい。 （日本大）

What has been the effect of current living wage laws?

① They have had no effect on local economies.

② They have been generally successful.

③ They have failed to improve people's lives.

④ They have not yet been clearly evaluated.

10.

テーマ　　国際
語　数　　489 words
出題校　　京都産業大

Born and raised on the very poor island of Makoko in Nigeria, Noah Shemede ⌾2-1 can still remember when he first held a bottle of Coca-Cola in his hand. He tasted the drink ten years ago, on his ninth birthday, after his parents had made a special trip just to buy a bottle of it for him. However, he did not enjoy that first mouthful.

5 "I thought it was awful," Noah said laughing.

(1)Across Africa, global brands like Coca-Cola were once rarely seen in places ⌾2-2 such as Makoko, where people were too poor to buy expensive brand-name goods. Now though, things are changing. Sub-Saharan Africa has experienced ten years of strong economic growth, and people's standard of living has risen as a result. The

10 brand-name goods that you can see in the supermarkets of rich countries are becoming more common. Big global companies expect Africa to keep on developing in the future.

Today, Noah Shemede's sister Fatima sells Coca-Cola, Fanta and Sprite, along ⌾2-3 with home-fried snacks, from her canoe. The price is still high for local people.

15 "These are not drinks for everyday drinking. Adults buy them for special occasions," she said. Another sign of change in Makoko that she tells us about is that families sometimes eat Nisshin instant noodles rather than traditional food like cow-tongue soup with rice.

All over the African continent, global companies interested in Africa's growth are ⌾2-4

20 trying to increase their sales. In Cameroon, Irish Guinness beer, famous for its rich flavor, has become an unexpected hit even in the countryside. Villagers like to mix it with local wine, to give it more taste and color. In Kenya and Nigeria, Samsung's solar-powered mobile phones are very popular. In Ivory Coast's cities, and even in the poor districts, (2)it is common to see youths selling Nestlé coffee in small cups,

25 so that locals can afford to buy some.

Swiss-based Nestlé, which is one of the biggest global coffee and sweets ⌾2-5 companies, has been very successful in Africa recently. One reason for this is that it has used local sales agents. The people who own the family-run shops, which are so common in Africa, prefer to deal with people they know. In this way, Nestlé has

30 doubled the number of African shops selling its products during the last year. Now, nearly half of its yearly profits come from developing countries, and Africa is an especially important market.

2-6　　This trend is not all positive. (3)<u>Not everyone thinks it is a good thing for the world's richest companies to make their profits in the world's poorest countries.</u> After all, these companies can damage local producers of similar products, and probably poor people would be better off spending their limited money on health, education, and technology rather than on costly brand-name products. But all the same, the increasing consumption of global brands does show that Africa is getting richer, and this can only be good for its many poor people.

35

1 下線部（1）について、その理由を日本語で答えなさい。

_____

2 下線部（2）を和訳しなさい。

_____

_____

3 下線部（3）を和訳しなさい。

_____

_____

4 本文の内容に最もよく合うものをそれぞれ1つずつ選びなさい。 〔京都産業大・改〕

(1) **The international companies are targeting Africa because _____ .**

①　the economy continues to grow there

②　local companies want to cooperate with them

③　the number of supermarkets has increased dramatically

④　their products are essential for the lives of African people

(2) **According to Fatima, Coca-Cola _____ .**

①　is not enjoyed daily

②　goes well with traditional food

③　is inexpensive if bought locally

④　is so special that adults will not drink it

(3) **One of the reasons Nestlé has hired many locals in Africa as salespeople is _____ .**

①　the cost of hiring local people is high

②　people would rather not do business with strangers

③　the company's treatment of local staff is outstanding

④　family-run shops there are more stable than supermarkets

(4) **What would be the best title for this passage?**

①　Africa: the Last Resort

②　Global Brands in Africa

③　Disadvantages of Global Brands

④　Where Global Brands Came From

11.

テーマ	自然
語　数	344 words
出題校	兵庫県立大

A coral reef★ is made up of many coral colonies all living together. The reef may ◉2-11 stretch hundreds of miles across, but it is constructed by coral polyps★ only a quarter of an inch or less in size. The reef itself is a living, growing organism — colonies of tiny animals all working together to create the largest structures on Earth. This is one of the most complex and mysterious ecosystems★ known to mankind, and it all works because of the tiny animals that produce the huge reef structure.

Over half a billion years ago, before there was any life on land, the seas contained ◉2-12 primitive coral reefs, consisting of sponges★ and primitive corals. (1)This means that coral reefs are among the oldest complex natural communities still in existence on Earth. While many changes and extinctions in reefs have occurred throughout their history, reefs have survived. In fact, some coral reef animals known today are almost unchanged from those found in fossils dating from the age of dinosaurs, 100 million years ago. (2)Coral reefs are wonderful to see, and rich gardens in the sea, supporting an astonishing amount of marine life in a densely packed, thriving marine metropolis. In fact, coral reefs have the largest abundance and greatest diversity of life living together of any place on Earth, including the tropical rain forests. (3)People often refer to coral reefs as "rainforests of the sea."

In an area with this much diversity of life, it is easy to think that the tropical ◉2-13 oceans are highly rich in nutrients. (4)This is the popular misunderstanding. Compared to the cold, murky waters of the temperate seas, tropical seas limit the number of animal plankton, which makes their water clear, yet with very low food resources. Thus, coral reefs live in nearly sterile★ water. A coral reef is a gathering place in the ocean. (5)It is an oasis in a desert, a place which gives shelter and food in an ocean where these things are rare. In fact, the entire tropical ocean ecosystem depends on the reef for sustenance.

> ★ reef「礁（しょう）」　coral polyps「サンゴ虫」　ecosystem「生態系」
> sponges「海綿動物」　sterile「不毛な」

1 下線部 (1) の This が指す内容を日本語で説明しなさい。

_____

_____

2 下線部 (2) を和訳しなさい。

_____

_____

3 下線部 (3) のように述べられている理由を最もよく表すものを 1 つ選びなさい。 (兵庫県立大)

① Strange creatures are often found in a tropical ocean.

② Numberless creatures make up a living organism.

③ Beauty of nature can be seen in the sea.

④ Living things in the sea have something in common with those in forests.

4 下線部 (4) に関して、次の① [   ] ② [   ] の空所に適切な日本語を入れなさい。

実際は、熱帯の海は ① [   ] のに、一般

の人々は ② [   ] と誤解している。

5 下線部 (5) の理由を最もよく表すものを 1 つ選びなさい。 (兵庫県立大)

① Fishes are always searching for food and shelter in the tropical ocean.

② Coral polyps produce clearer water for their growth.

③ There are few living creatures in the tropical ocean except coral polyps.

④ There are almost no other places to feed and protect sea animals.

6 本文のタイトルとして最もふさわしいものを 1 つ選びなさい。 (兵庫県立大)

① Coral Reefs — How to Enjoy Summer in the Ocean

② The Wonder of the Sea — A Number of Colonies

③ Searching for Beautiful Rainforests of the Sea

④ Tropical Ocean Ecosystem — The Life of Coral Reefs

12.

テーマ	動物
語 数	432 words
出題校	名古屋工業大

For some lizards it is easy being green. It is in their blood. Six species of lizards in ⏺2-18 New Guinea bleed lime green thanks to evolution gone weird. It is unusual, but there are creatures that bleed different colors of the rainbow besides red. The New Guinea lizards' blood — along with their tongues, muscles, and bones — appears green because of incredibly large doses of a green bile★ pigment★. ₍₁₎The bile levels are higher than those at which other animals, including people, could survive.

Scientists still do not know why this happened, but evolution is providing some ⏺2-19 hints into this nearly 50-year mystery. By mapping the evolutionary family tree of New Guinea lizards, researchers found that green blood developed inside the amphibians — animals that can live both on land and in water — at four independent points in history, likely from a red-blooded ancestor, according to a study in Wednesday's journal *Science Advances*. ₍₂₎This is not a random accident of nature but suggests this trait of green blood gives the lizards an evolutionary advantage of some kind, said Christopher Austin of Louisiana State University. "Evolution can do amazing things given enough time," Austin said. "The natural world is a fascinating place."

Austin first thought that maybe being green and full of bile would make New ⏺2-20 Guinea lizards taste bad to potential predators. "I actually ate several lizards myself and they did not taste bad," Austin said. He also fed plenty of them to a paradise kingfisher bird with no ill effects except maybe a fatter bird.

Understanding bile is probably key. Blood cells do not last forever. After they ⏺2-21 break down, the iron is recycled for new red blood cells, but toxins are also produced, which is essentially bile. In the New Guinea lizards, levels of a green bile pigment are 40 times higher than what would be toxic in humans. It is green enough to overwhelm the color of the red blood cells and (A) everything green, Austin said. In people, elevated green bile pigment levels sometimes kill malaria parasites. Austin thinks that might be why lizards evolved to be green-blooded because malaria is an issue for New Guinea and lizards. It might be the result of evolution trying to kill the malaria parasite in lizards or it might be past lizards were infected so heavily that this was the body's reaction, he said.

Michael Oellermann, a researcher at the University of Tasmania in Australia, ⏺2-22 praised Austin's work and wondered if there is an evolutionary cost to having green blood. (3)Otherwise more creatures would bleed green or another color, he said.

* bile「胆汁」　pigment「色素」

1 下線部（1）を和訳しなさい。

_____

_____

2 下線部（2）This の具体的な内容を、本文に即して日本語で説明しなさい。

_____

_____

3 本文中の空所（A）に入る最も適切な語を 1 つ選びなさい。　(名古屋工業大)

①　appear　　　②　deserve　　　③　perceive　　　④　turn

4 下線部（3）を、Otherwise の表す内容を明らかにしながら和訳しなさい。

_____

_____

_____

5 本文の内容に一致するものを 1 つ選びなさい。

①　It is common for people in New Guinea to eat lizards to prevent disease.

②　Some researchers examined trees in New Guinea and found some hints to solving the mystery of the green blood.

③　It has become clear that the lizards' green blood helped them avoid and kill their predators.

④　Malaria parasites are weak against blood with very high bile pigment levels.

13.

テーマ　歴史
語　数　385 words
出題校　東邦大

Since ancient times, historians have noticed that the rise and fall of civilizations is ⊘2-27 closely connected to population changes. These shifts in population have had (1)a significant effect on the destiny of societies. Shrinking populations have often given way militarily, economically, and culturally to expanding populations. Growing
5 populations, particularly when geographically bound, have been the cause of many historical events. Among the historical changes brought about by population growth are political revolutions and national expansion.

Britain's expansion into the New World and the Industrial Revolution were both in ⊘2-28 many ways the result of Great Britain's large population growth rates in the 17th
10 century. (2)Britain's population growth resulted in a widely held belief in the 18th and 19th centuries that it faced an unemployment crisis. To resolve the crisis, the government encouraged people to move abroad to its colonies in America and Australia. It also encouraged businesses to invest in new ideas as a way of creating jobs. Some of the new ideas eventually led to the technological breakthroughs of the Industrial
15 Revolution.

Population growth in 18th-century France played a role in the French Revolution. ⊘2-29 France's population grew from 24.6 million in 1740 to 28.1 million in 1790. This helped increase the demand for food at a time of short supply, thereby driving up food prices throughout France. Price rises spread further as a result of urbanization and
20 the increased circulation of money. Consequently, (3)the purchasing power of the average French wage earner was reduced, which caused a business downturn. The downturn hurt the growing and increasingly powerful French craftsman and merchant classes. This situation led to social unrest made worse by an unfair tax system, which failed to provide enough revenue to support public spending. This in turn led to
25 financial ruin in 1787 and finally revolution in 1789.

Japanese expansion from the 1870s to 1945 was caused in part by Japan's rise in ⊘2-30 population. In the mid-19th century, the Japanese population grew rapidly. This came after a period of 150 years in which Japanese deliberately reduced their birth rates to slow growth. Growth led to fears about declining living standards and the need for
30 more land. Japanese rulers took advantage of (4)these fears and gathered support for an expansionist policy. This included settling the northern islands of the archipelago and taking control of Okinawa, Taiwan and Korea.

1 下線部（1）が指すものを、第1段落の内容を踏まえて、日本語で説明しなさい。

_____

_____

_____

2 下線部（2）を和訳しなさい。

_____

_____

3 下線部（3）を和訳しなさい。

_____

_____

4 下線部（4）の内容を、日本語で答えなさい。

_____

5 次の各問の答えとして最も適切なものを1つずつ選びなさい。　　　　　　(東邦大)

(1) Who was encouraged to relocate (move to another place) in the 19th century?

① The British government. 　　② Americans and Australians.

③ The British population. 　　④ British businesses.

(2) How did population growth lead to the French Revolution?

① It made the craftsman and merchant classes more powerful.

② It increased the demand for food, which caused inflation.

③ It led to more public spending and eventual economic failure.

④ It caused urban areas to grow, which led to social unrest.

(3) When did Japanese intentionally reduce their birth rates?

① From the 18th to the mid-19th century.

② From the mid-19th century until 1945.

③ From the 19th to the mid-20th century.

④ From the 1870s for a period of 150 years.

14.

テーマ	科学
語　数	409 words
出題校	神奈川大

　　Most people know that the *Titanic* sank because it hit an iceberg*. However, ◉2-35 Donald Olson, an expert in physics, and a team of scientists have examined (1)the role the moon may have played in the disaster. Since the *Titanic* sank in the early hours of April 15, 1912, resulting in great loss of life, scholars have puzzled over why 5 Captain Edward Smith was not worried about warnings of icebergs nearby. Smith, the most experienced captain in the White Star Line, had sailed the North Atlantic sea lanes on numerous occasions. He had been assigned to the first voyage of the *Titanic* because he was a knowledgeable and careful seaman.

　　Why had such a large number of icebergs floated into the shipping lanes so far ◉2-36 10 south that night? Olson and his team investigated one theory that an unusually close approach by the moon in January, 1912 may have produced very high tides. As a result, far more icebergs than usual managed to separate from Greenland, and floated, still fully grown, south into the shipping lanes.

　　Olson said (2)a "once in many lifetimes" event occurred on January 4, 1912, when ◉2-37 15 the moon and sun lined up in such a way that their gravitational pulls* increased each other. At the same time, the moon's approach to Earth that January was the closest it had been in 1,400 years. The point of closest approach occurred within six minutes of the full moon. (3)On top of that, the Earth's closest approach to the sun in a year had happened just the previous day. "This (4)arrangement of events increased 20 the moon's tide-raising power to the maximum," Olson said. Olson's research determined that to reach the shipping lanes by mid-April, (5)(must / the *Titanic* / that / the iceberg / into / have / crashed) broken off from Greenland in January, 1912. The high tide caused by the strange combination of events would have been enough to separate icebergs and keep them floating to reach the shipping lanes by April, he 25 said.

　　(6)The team's *Titanic* research may justify Captain Smith's choices by showing ◉2-38 that he had a good excuse for reacting so casually to a report of ice in the ship's path. He had no reason at the time to believe that the icebergs he was facing were as numerous or as large as they turned out to be, Olson said.

30 　　"The probability of all these variables lining up in just the way they did was, well, hard to imagine," he concluded.

　　* iceberg「氷山」　gravitational pulls「引力」

1 下線部（1）について、その具体的な内容を本文に即して日本語で説明しなさい。

_____

_____

2 下線部（2）はどのような意味か、次の中から最も適切なものを 1 つ選びなさい。

① 多くの命が失われた出来事　　　② 何世代にもわたって完成された事業

③ 何千年に一度の出来事　　　　　④ 何人もの人々がかつて経験した出来事

3 下線部（3）（4）の内容の説明として最も適切なものを 1 つずつ選びなさい。　　（神奈川大）

(3) **On top of**

① In addition to　　　　　　② Positioned just above

③ Supported by　　　　　　 ④ Immediately before

(4) **arrangement of events**

① gathering of parties　　　② schedule of actions

③ assembly of people　　　 ④ combination of factors

4 下線部（5）の（　　）内の語句を正しく並べかえなさい。

_____

5 下線部（6）を和訳しなさい。

_____

_____

6 次の（1）〜（3）の英文に続けるのに最も適切なものを 1 つずつ選びなさい。　　（神奈川大・改）

(1) **Captain Edward Smith was assigned to the _Titanic_ because**

① he was president of the White Star Line at that time.

② he had spent many years crossing the Atlantic Ocean.

③ he was the oldest captain commanding White Star Line ships.

④ he was interested in icebergs and wished to study their movements.

(2) **Olson believes Captain Smith may have reacted calmly to the report of icebergs because ...**

① the _Titanic_ was built so that it would never sink.

② he thought they would be smaller and fewer than they actually were.

③ he heard that only a few very small icebergs were floating in the area.

④ the reports said the icebergs were very dangerous for the _Titanic_.

(3) **According to Olson, the chances of such an accident happening would have been ...**

① planned in great detail.　　　② pictured clearly.

③ difficult to predict.　　　　　④ scientifically mapped.

15.

テーマ　教育
語　数　367 words
出題校　専修大

In junior high school, one of my classmates had a TV addiction★ — back before ◉2-43
it was normal. This boy — we'll call him Ethan — watched TV all day long and
knew almost everything about TV comic shows.

Then one day, Ethan's mother made him (1)a bold offer. If he could go a full
5　month without watching any TV, she would give him $200. None of us thought he
could do it. But Ethan quit TV quite easily. His friends offered to let him (2)cheat
at their houses on Friday nights. Ethan said no. One month later, Ethan's mom paid
him $200. He went out and bought a TV, the biggest one he could find.

Since there have been children, there have been adults trying to get them to obey ◉2-44
10　their parents. The Bible repeatedly commands children to listen to their parents and
proposes that disobedient★ children be killed by throwing stones at them, or at least
have their eyes picked out by cruel birds. Over the centuries, (3)the stick has lost favor
to the carrot in most cases. Today adults start rewarding kids with cheap gifts, such
as a candy for using the toilet or a cookie for sitting still in church, before kids can
15　speak in full sentences.

In recent years, hundreds of schools in the USA have made these transactions ◉2-45
more businesslike, experimenting with paying kids with real money for showing up
in class, getting good grades or going another day without fighting.

I have not met a child who does not admire this trend. But (4)it makes adults ◉2-46
20　terribly uncomfortable. Teachers complain that we are rewarding kids for doing what
they should be doing of their own will. Psychologists warn that money can actually
make kids perform worse, because it makes them lose respect for the act of learning.
Parents predict that kids will be lazy after the incentives go away. (5)The debate has
become a big battle that caused the larger dispute over why our kids are not learning at
25　the rate they should be despite decades of reforms and budget increases.

But all this time, there has been only one real question, particularly in America's ◉2-47
lowest-performing schools: Does it work?

★ addiction「中毒」　disobedient「言うことをきかない」

1 下線部（1）の具体的な内容を日本語で答えなさい。

_____

2 下線部（2）は具体的に何をすることを表しているか、日本語で答えなさい。

_____

3 下線部（3）の意味として最も適切なものを1つ選びなさい。 (専修大)

① 罰よりも報酬を与えるほうが好まれるようになった。

② 敗者はほうびではなく罰を与えられた。

③ ほうびのアメもなめると味がなくなり、ただの棒になった。

④ 子どもに石を投げつけると、現代社会では罰せられる。

4 下線部（4）について、教師たちはどのように考えているのか、日本語で答えなさい。

_____

_____

5 下線部（5）を和訳しなさい。

_____

_____

6 本文の内容に一致するものを1つ選びなさい。 (専修大)

① Kids may respond better to rewards for specific actions because there is less risk of failure.

② Most of the kids work hard for the love of learning, not for short-term rewards.

③ A combination of school reforms and the interaction among those reforms will matter more than any single change in isolation.

④ Some schools in the USA give kids money when they get good grades.

7 本文のタイトルとして最も適当なものを1つ選びなさい。 (専修大)

① Should Kids Be Given Money to Do Well in School?

② How Ethan Spends Friday Nights with His Friends

③ Kids Can Learn More than They Should with Friends

④ Money Always Makes Kids Perform Worse in School

16.

テーマ　技術
語　数　610 words
出題校　岩手大

The number of road deaths in Japan in 2018 was a record low of 3,532. The 〇2-52
National Police Agency reported that this reduction since the peak in 1970 of over
16,000 was due to more traffic safety education. The introduction of seat belts, air
bags and other safety equipment into cars since 1970 is also likely to be a factor.
5　Three thousand five hundred is still a high number, averaging roughly ten per day.
Many people dream that self-driving cars (SDC) will greatly increase road safety. To
date, the accidents involving SDCs have been caused by humans. The hope is that
when all cars are SDCs, human error will be (A)eradicated, and road deaths become
a thing of the past.

10　However pleasant this idea may be, it remains a dream. SDCs need to be 〇2-53
programmed to predict as many situations as possible to reduce danger. Certainly,
unexpected situations will still occur, such as people breaking the law at red lights
and walking into the oncoming traffic. A major question arises; when danger cannot
be circumvented, how should SDCs be programmed to respond?

15　The English philosopher Phillipa Foot introduced a thought experiment called 〇2-54
the *Trolley Problem*. A driverless train is going along a track which divides into two
branches. On one branch, five people are tied up on the track. On the other branch,
one person is tied up. The train cannot be stopped, and it will hit the five people. A
switch controls which branch the train travels. You have (1)two options: 1) to press
20　the switch to move the train onto the other track. This means that one person will
be hit, but that you will have initiated this; 2) to do nothing. In this case, five people
will be hit, but you will not be involved in the accident. In tests, most people *say* that
they will press the switch and save five lives.

The Trolley Problem is useful for future SDC technology because it gets people 〇2-55
25　to think about issues that are important in road safety. Should SDCs be programmed
to, for example, save more or fewer lives? The options can be changed to other
choices. Should young people's lives be saved instead of old people's? Females or
males? Doctors or homeless people? Healthy or unhealthy? The list goes on. A
team of scientists from the Massachusetts Institute of Technology (MIT) created a
30　website to ask these questions. By 2018, the MIT team had collected over 40 million
responses from all over the world. The results were (B)intriguing: females are more
important than males; younger people more valuable than older people; high-status

citizens more meaningful than low-status individuals. Differences between cultures were also observed. For example, Eastern countries, including Japan, preferred to (2-1) the (2-2) of lawful people, but Southern countries, such as Brazil, did not. ₃₅

2-56   So far, however, these tests are only thought experiments. (3)<u>What people *say* they will do and what they *actually* do may be very different.</u> What we say is based on how we *think*. But are we *really* the people we think we are? In 2018, an American TV show *Mind Field* tested this question with real people. Making this show was very dangerous in terms of morals because it can cause severe psychological damage to ₄₀ the people in the study. The information learned from the show, however, indicated that many people would be paralyzed; they could do nothing. The message for SDCs is highly complex. From now on, there needs to be a serious discussion between governments, car manufacturers and consumer groups about how SDCs should respond to unusual situations. (4)<u>This</u> is likely to be an intriguing and extremely ₄₅ valuable discussion.

1   Which is the closest in meaning to each of the underlined words (A) and (B)?   (岩手大)

(A) eradicated
   ① destroyed   ② removed   ③ defeated   ④ damaged
(B) intriguing
   ① disappointing   ② frightening   ③ interesting   ④ encouraging

2   Regarding the underlined part (1), explain in Japanese what the result will be if you choose the option 2).

_____

3   Write the most appropriate word to fill in each of the blank spaces (2-1) and (2-2). Choose the words from the passage.

(2-1) _____
(2-2) _____

4   Translate the underlined part (3) into Japanese.

_____

→次頁へ

5 Regarding the underlined word (4), explain in Japanese what "This" refers to.

_____

_____

6 Choose one statement that is true according to the passage. (岩手大・改)

① The reason for accidents with SDCs so far is because of faulty programming.

② In the *Trolley Problem* a train can be made to avoid hitting people.

③ According to the MIT study, many people think that doctors are more important than homeless people.

④ In the TV show *Mind Field*, most people chose to save the lives of more people than a few people.

Memo

17.

テーマ　　睡眠
語　数　　529 words
出題校　　京都産業大学

We often worry about lying awake in the middle of the night — but it may not ❂ 2-61 be a problem. A growing body of evidence from both science and history suggests that a long and uninterrupted sleep may not be natural.

In the early 1990s, researcher Thomas Wehr conducted (1)an experiment in which ❂ 2-62 a group of people were kept in darkness for 14 hours every day for a month. It took some time for their sleep to become regular, but by the fourth week the subjects had settled into a very distinct sleeping pattern. They slept first for four hours, then woke for one or two hours before falling into a second four-hour sleep.

(2)Though sleep scientists paid attention to the results of the study, the idea that ❂ 2-63 we must sleep for eight continuous hours persists among the general public. More recently, in 2001, historian Roger Ekirch of Virginia Tech published an influential paper, drawn from 16 years of research, revealing a lot of historical evidence that humans used to sleep in two distinct periods. His book *At Day's Close: Night in Times Past*, published four years later, presents more than 500 references to (3)a split sleeping pattern — in diaries, court records, medical books, and literature, from ancient Greece to modern Africa.

Much like the experience of Wehr's subjects, these references describe a first sleep ❂ 2-64 which began about two hours after sunset, followed by a waking period of one or two hours and then a second sleep. "It's not just the number of references to this sleeping pattern that is significant, but it's also the way they refer to it, as if it were common knowledge," Ekirch says.

During this waking period, people did all kinds of things. They often got up, ❂ 2-65 went to the toilet or smoked tobacco and some even visited neighbors. People read, wrote, and often prayed. Countless prayer manuals from the late 15th century offered special prayers for the hours in between sleeps. Ekirch found that references to the first and second sleep began to disappear during the late 17th century. (4)This started among the urban upper classes in northern Europe, and over the course of the next 200 years gradually influenced the rest of Western society. By the 1920s, the idea of a first and second sleep had disappeared completely.

Ekirch gives the reasons for the initial shift as improvements in street lighting, ❂ 2-66 home lighting and an increase in coffee houses, which were sometimes open all night.

(5)As the night became a time for increased activity, the length of time people could spend resting decreased. With the introduction of street lighting, socializing at night slowly became common among all social classes. In 1667, Paris became the first city in the world to light its streets, using wax candles in glass lamps. It was followed by Amsterdam two years later, where a much more efficient oil-powered lamp was developed. London did not install street lighting until 1684, but by the end of the century, more than 50 of Europe's major towns and cities were lit at night. Nighttime activities became fashionable, so people went to bed later, and (　6　).

35

1 下線部（1）の実験の最終的な結果を、日本語で簡潔に説明しなさい。

_____

_____

2 下線部（2）を和訳しなさい。

_____

_____

3 下線部（3）の内容を表すものとして最も適当なものを 1 つ選びなさい。

① A pattern of sleeping that is good for health

② A pattern of sleeping that harmed people in the past

③ A pattern of sleeping uninterrupted for long hours

④ A pattern of sleeping with two parts

4 下線部（4）の This が示す内容を日本語で答えなさい。

_____

_____

5 下線部（5）を和訳しなさい。

_____

_____

→次頁へ

6 空所（6）に入れるのに最も適切なものを 1 つ選びなさい。

① gradually lost interest in socializing

② only had one period of sleep

③ back to their former sleeping pattern

④ woke up in the middle of the night

7 本文の内容に一致するものをすべて選びなさい。 （京都産業大・改）

① Wehr asked the subjects to sleep in different patterns from each other in his experiment.

② Ekirch included references in his book to prove the benefits of continuous sleep.

③ Many references in Ekirch's book suggest that people long ago found a divided sleeping pattern normal.

④ In the past, during the nighttime waking period, people engaged in personal and social activities.

Memo

18.

テーマ　心理
語　数　605 words
出題校　甲南大

There is (1)a paradox★ at the heart of our lives. Most people want more income ⊘2-71 and work hard for it. Yet, as Western societies have got richer, their people have become no happier. This is no old wives' tale. It is a fact proven by many pieces of scientific research. As I'll show, we have good ways to measure how happy people are, and all the evidence says that on average people are no happier today than people were fifty years ago. At the same time, however, average incomes have doubled. This paradox is equally true for the United States, Britain and Japan.

But aren't our lives infinitely more comfortable? Indeed: we have more food, ⊘2-72 more clothes, more cars, more holidays and, above all, better health. Yet we are not happier. Despite all the efforts of governments, teachers and doctors which have improved our lives, human happiness has not increased. Suppose you were asked to choose between living in two imaginary worlds, in which prices were the same. In the first of these worlds you would get $50,000 a year, compared with an average income of $25,000. In the second of these worlds you would get $100,000 a year, compared with an average income of $250,000. Which do you choose? This question was put to a group of Harvard students and (2)the majority preferred the first type of world. They were happy to be poorer, if their relative position improved. People care greatly about their relative income, and they would be willing to accept a significant fall as long as they could improve their position in relation to other people.

People also compare their income with what they themselves are used to. When ⊘2-73 they are asked how much income they need, richer people always say they need more than poorer people. So (3)whether you are happy with your income depends on how it compares with some standard. And that standard depends on two things: what other people get and what you yourself are accustomed to getting. In the first case your feelings are governed by social comparison, and in the second by your ability to get used to things.

2-74　　Because these two forces are so strong in human nature, it is quite difficult for economic growth to improve our happiness.　The reason for this is that as actual incomes rise, the standard by which income is judged rises in step.　You can see this ₃₀ from data collected by the Gallup Poll★ in the United States over many years.　People were asked, "What is the smallest amount of money a family of four needs to get along reasonably well in this community?　" (4)The chart shows how much money people thought they needed to live comfortably — that is, their "required income," and how much money they actually earn — that is, their "actual income."　According to the ₃₅ chart, as people's actual income increases, the amount of money they say they need also increases.　So even though people become richer, they are never satisfied.　They never say, "I earn much more than I need, so I am happy."　They simply feel that they need more money to be happy.　This explains why people become no happier even when their standard of living improves. ₄₀

2-75　　These facts are truly depressing, because they mean that (5)we cannot be happier however much money we might get.　But at the same time, they teach us a useful lesson: financial success is not always necessary for your happiness, and to find another aspect of life that satisfies you is an easier way of becoming happy.

　　　　★　paradox「逆説」　Gallup Poll「ギャラップ調査（世論調査の一種)」

1　第1段落の内容を踏まえて、下線部（1）の a paradox の具体的な内容を日本語で簡潔に答えなさい。

_____

_____

2　下線部（2）について、なぜこのような結果になったのかを日本語で説明しなさい。

_____

_____

3　下線部（3）を和訳しなさい。

_____

_____

→次頁へ

4 下線部（4）が指す図表として最も適切なものを次の中から選びなさい。
（甲南大）

A.

B.
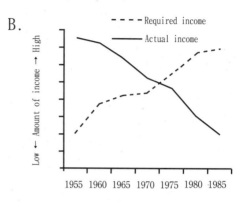

C.
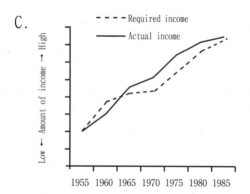

D.
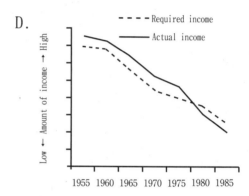

5 下線部（5）を和訳しなさい。

---

6 本文の内容と一致するものを 2 つ選びなさい。
（甲南大）

① It is hard to say that we are happier than people were 50 years ago.

② We don't feel happier than we did 50 years ago because our standard of living has not improved.

③ Most people are not interested in the income of other people.

④ People's "actual income" is the amount of money people actually want.

⑤ Money is not a definite route to happiness.

MEMO

MEMO

MEMO

MEMO

Chapter 1

▶ Union of Concerned Scientists

憂慮する科学者同盟（略称 UCS）。1969 年に設立された非営利団体で、全世界約 9 万人の市民と科学者からの寄付だけで運営されている。本部は米国ボストンにあり、より清潔で健康的な環境と、より安全な世界を築くための活動を行っている。核兵器の廃絶、原子力発電の安全性向上、自然エネルギーの推進、気候変動への対応など、幅広いジャンルの提言を行っている。

▶ water

人間が消費する食品や工業製品を生産するのに必要な水の総量を「ウォーター・フットプリント（Water Footprint）」という。生産時だけではなく、流通、廃棄するときの水の使用量までを含めて算出されることが多い。オランダの国際 NGO である「ウォーター・フットプリント・ネットワーク」が独自に算定した結果が広く知られている。

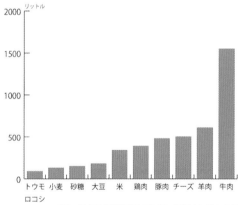

100g 当たりの農畜産物の生産に使用される水の量

▶ livestock

家畜。人間が肉や卵、皮、労働力などを利用するために飼育している動物。牛や豚、馬、ヤギなどのほ乳類、またはニワトリなどの鳥類を指すことが一般的だが、ミツバチやカイコなどの昆虫を含める場合もある。

国連食糧農業機関によれば、地球の地表面積の約 30％が家畜の飼育に利用されている。1970 年以降、ブラジルのアマゾンの熱帯雨林の約 15％が、牧草地への転用を目的とする森林伐採によって消滅した。

1999 年における世界の肉の生産量は 2 億 2,900 万トンだったが、2050 年には約 2 倍の 4 億 6,500 万トンになると予想されている。

▶ methane

メタンガス。メタンガスが大気中に存在する量は二酸化炭素の約 200 分の 1 程度だが、大気中の熱を蓄える効果は二酸化炭素の約 21 〜 25 倍に及ぶ。また、大気中で安定して存在している期間は約 12 年（二酸化炭素は約 100 年）である。

各国に比べ、日本のメタンガスの排出量が少ないのは、農畜産業の生産量が少ないことが理由の 1 つである。

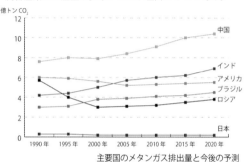

主要国のメタンガス排出量と今後の予測

▶ greenhouse gas

温室効果ガス。地表から放射された熱を吸収し、その一部を下向きに放射する性質を持つ気体の総称。二酸化炭素やメタン、一酸化二窒素、フロンなど。

2014 年 11 月、IPCC（気候変動に関する政府間パネル）は、産業革命以前の平均気温の＋ 2 度以内に抑えるために今後排出できる二酸化炭素の総量は 1 兆トンであると発表した。2011 年の全世界の二酸化炭素排出量約 318 億トンで計算すると、32 年で 1 兆トンを超えることになる。産業革命以降の 300 年間弱で放出された二酸化炭素の総量が 1.9 兆トンであることからも、近年の排出量がどれほど多いかがわかる。

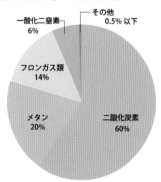

産業革命以降人為的に排出された温室効果ガスの地球温暖化への寄与度

Chapter 2

▶ **vegan diet**

　ヴィーガン・ダイエット（完全菜食主義の食事）。穀物や豆類、種実類、野菜、果物、またそれらを加工したパンやパスタ、豆腐、蕎麦などを中心とした、乳製品や卵を含む動物性食品を一切含まない食事。完全菜食主義者は、植物性食物から摂取できないビタミン B12 などの栄養素はシリアルなどで摂取する。アップル創業者のスティーブ・ジョブズ氏が完全菜食主義者として知られている。

　vegetarian は、動物由来の卵や牛乳は口にする「卵乳菜食主義者」などを含む広義の菜食主義者全般を指すことが多い。

▶ **Institute of Medicine**

　米国医学研究所。略称は IOM。米国科学アカデミー（The National Academy of America）の健康等について研究する部門として 1970 年に設立された。政府から独立した非営利団体で、健康等についての情報を発信し、国民の健康増進を図っている。

▶ **caffeine**

　カフェイン。アルカロイドという化合物の一種で、コーヒーやお茶、コーラ、ココアなどの食品に含まれている。覚醒・解熱・鎮痛作用があることから、栄養ドリンクや感冒薬（かぜ薬）などに広く用いられている。また、腎臓の血管を拡張し、多くの血液をろ過し、水分とともに老廃物を体外へ排出する利尿作用もある。

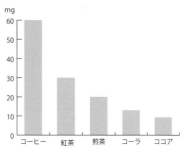

100ml あたりに含まれるカフェイン量

▶ **National Academy of Science**

　米国化学アカデミー。略称は NAS。南北戦争中の 1863 年、リンカーン大統領によって設立された科学者団体。これまでに約 200 人の会員がノーベル賞を受賞している。2014 年時点の会員数は、米国人約 2,200 人、外国人が約 400 人。会員の選出基準が非常に厳格であることから、世界中の科学者にとって会員に選ばれることは最も名誉なことの 1 つとされている。これまでに iPS 細胞の研究でノーベル賞を受賞した山中伸弥氏をはじめ 49 人の日本人が会員に選出されている。

Chapter 3

▸ Old English

古英語（古期英語）。およそ450〜1150年頃までの英語。5世紀頃からイングランドを侵略、支配したゲルマン民族が持ち込んだ言語で、アングロ・サクソン語とも呼ばれる。現在の英国の中心的な島であるグレートブリテン島には、ゲルマン人が侵略する前まではケルト人が住んでいて、主な言語はケルト語だった。以下は8〜9世紀頃の作品で、古英語で記されている『ベオウルフ（Beowulf）』の冒頭の一節。

【原文】

Hwæt, wē Gār-Dena in geārdagum, þēodcyninga þrym gefrunon, hū ðā æþelingas ellen fremedon.

【現代英語訳】

LO, praise of the prowess of people-kings of spear-armed Danes, in days long sped, we have heard, and what honor the athelings won!

【日本語訳】（忍足欣四郎『ベーオウルフ』岩波書店より）

いざ聞き給え、そのかみの槍の誉れ高きデネ人（びと）の勲（いさおし）、民の王たる人々の武名は、貴人（あてびと）らが天晴れ勇武の振舞をなせし次第は、語り継がれてわれらが耳に及ぶところとなった。

■ 参考：唯一現存する『ベオウルフ』の写本（大英博物館）

▸ Middle English

中英語（中世英語）。およそ1150〜1500年頃の英語。1066年にノルマン人に征服されたイングランドでは、ノルマン人が話していた中世フランス語が大量に流入した。フランス語から持ち込まれた単語は1万を超え、約7,500語は今も残っている。

▸ Modern English

近代英語。一般的には1500〜1650年頃までの初期近代英語と、それ以降の後期近代英語に分けられる。William Shakespeare（シェイクスピア：1564 - 1616）の作品が初期近代英語の代表的な文献である。この時点では、vとuに違いがないといったようにアルファベットの使われ方が今とは異なり、つづりも確定していなかった。

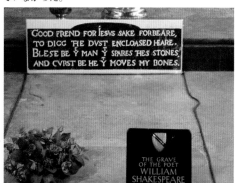

■ 参考：初期近代英語で書かれたシェイクスピアの墓碑

【現代英語訳】

Good friend, for Jesus' sake forbear, To dig the dust enclosed here. Blest be the man that spares these stones, But cursed be he that moves my bones.

【日本語訳】

良き友よ、願わくば（＝イエスにかけて）、ここに葬られし遺骸を掘りおこすことなかれ。これらの墓石に触れざる者に恵みあらんことを。わが骨を動かす者に呪いあれ。

▸ Noah Webster

ノア・ウェブスター（1758 - 1843）。米国の辞書編纂者。エール大学卒業後の1783〜1785年に、つづりや文法規則をまとめた *A Grammatical Institute of the English Language*『英語文法提要』を出版し、その一部である『アメリカつづり字教科書』は以降100年間にわたって米国の教育現場で使われ続けた。その後、米国内で統一されていなかったつづりや発音の標準化を目指して辞書の編纂を始め、1828年に *An American Dictionary of English Language*『アメリカ英語辞書』を出版した。

辞書の編纂にあたっては、数多くのつづりの改革を行った。英国で「色」を意味するcolourが米国ではcolorと表記されるようになったのは、ウェブスターの改革によるものである。

Chapter 4

▶ artificial intelligence

　人工知能（AI）。人間の脳が行っている知的作業を、コンピューターで模倣したソフトウェアやシステムのこと。通常の機械やロボット等と決定的に異なる点は、人工知能を搭載した機械等は「自ら思考し、学習できる」点である。今後、人工知能研究が発展することで、今ある職業の多くが、彼らに取って替わられるという予測がある。

▶ Martine Rothblatt

　マーティン・ロスブラット。1954 年生まれのアメリカの女性起業家。カリフォルニア大学ロサンゼルス校（UCLA）を 1981 年に卒業した後、通信衛星法に関する法律事務所の弁護士となる。しかし、通信衛星分野に商機を見出した彼女は、2 年後の 1983 年に法律事務所を退職。同年、衛星ナビゲーションによるカーナビシステムの会社、ジオスター社を創設する。また、1990 年には、通信衛星システムによるラジオ放送を提供する、シリウス・サテライト・ラジオ社を起業する。1996 年、娘の難病治療のために、製薬会社であるユナイデット・セラピューティクス社を立ち上げ、現在同社の会長を務めている。28 歳のときに妻であるビーナ氏と結婚。マーティン氏は 40 歳のとき、トランスジェンダーであることを告白し、男性から女性に性転換している。

▶ Bina48

　ビーナ 48。マーティン氏の配偶者であるビーナ氏をモデルとしたロボット。ビーナ氏が 48 歳のときに製作されたことが名前の由来。マーティン氏はこのロボットの開発のために、2010 年にハンソン・ロボティクス社を設立。ビーナ氏への 20 時間に渡るインタビューを元にした人工知能が搭載されている。

▶ mind clones

　頭脳クローン。マーティン氏によれば、「頭脳ファイル（mind file）」と呼ばれる「その人の特徴、個性、記憶、感情、信条、態度、価値観や、SNS 内での発言や投稿など、その人に関する全ての情報を集積したファイル」を元に作られた脳のコピーのことを指す。こうしたクローンは、オリジナルの人間からは独立した思考や感覚、記憶を持ち、独自に行動、判断、学習することができると、マーティン氏は考えている。

▶ Ray Kurzweil

　レイ・カーツワイル。1948 年生まれ。アメリカ合衆国の発明家、実業家、未来学者。マサチューセッツ工科大学（MIT）出身。人工知能研究の世界的権威であり、2012 年にグーグル社に入社。2005 年の著作『シンギュラリティは近い』（原題：*Singulaity is Near*）内で「2029 年にコンピューターの知能が完全に人間を超す」、「2040 年代には人々は仮想現実の中で大半を過ごすようになる」などの未来予測を展開している。

▶ Transhuman

　トランスヒューマン。新しい科学技術を用いて、身体能力や認知能力を進化させ、標準的な人間の能力を超えた人間のこと。SF 作品などに時折登場する、サイボーグや遺伝的に強化された人間が、トランスヒューマンである。

Chapter 5

▶ **quagga**

　クアッガ、またはクアッハとも。ウマ目ウマ科ウマ属サバンナシマウマの一亜種。クアッガという名前は、その鳴き声に由来している。特徴的な縞模様はウマとの交配によってできたものではなく、クアッガ独自のもの。食用や革を目的とした乱獲により、1800 年代後半に絶滅した。

クアッガのはく製

▶ **zebra**

　シマウマ。哺乳鋼ウマ目ウマ科ウマ属のなかで、白黒の縞模様を持つ系統。草食動物。縞模様の効果については、草原のなかで天敵から身を守るための保護色であるとするものや、仲間同士で群れを見つけやすくするためのものなど、諸説存在する。

▶ **Southern Africa**

　南部アフリカ。アフリカ大陸を 5 つに分けた際の、最も南の地域を指す。大半がステップ気候に属する。南アフリカ共和国（Republic of South Africa / South Africa）との混同に注意。

▶ **plains zebra**

　サバンナシマウマ。シマウマ 3 系統のうちの 1 つで、残りの 2 つはヤマシマウマとグレビーシマウマ。分類上、サバンナシマウマは 6 種類の亜種に分かれ、クアッガはその亜種のうちの 1 種。

▶ **endangered animals**

　絶滅の危険にさらされている動物。国際自然保護連合（IUCN）が作成した「絶滅のおそれのある野生生物のリスト」（通称、レッドリスト）によると、絶滅の危険性が高いとされる Threatened「絶滅危機種」のカテゴリーに分類された野生生物の数は、2019 年現在で約 2 万 8 千種にものぼる。

Chapter 7

▶ **pre-cooking ancestors**

　火の使用の開始時期については 170 万年前から 20 万年前までの広い範囲での説が唱えられており、いつ人類が調理に火を使い始めたのかについても正確にはわかっていない。人類が最初に手にした火は、落雷による森林火災などの自然現象によるものだと考えられている。

　火の使用により、人類は栄養を摂取しやすくなった。火を使わない頃の人類にとって、生肉を食べることは難しかった。なぜなら人類の歯の形状は生で肉を食べるには適しておらず、消化器官も不向きであったからだ。火の使用によって肉を加熱調理して摂取することが可能になり、加えて繊維質の多い種皮なども調理により食べることができるようになった。

▶ **apes**

　尾のない猿（無尾猿）。尾のある猿（有尾猿）はmonkey として区別されている。ヒト、チンパンジー、ゴリラ、オランウータンが無尾猿に含まれる。ニホンザルは有尾猿。

▶ **naked apes**

　毛のないサル。naked は「毛のない、裸の」という意味。イギリスの動物学者デズモンド・モリス（Desmond Morris）の著書に『裸のサル』がある。原題は「The Naked Ape」。

Chapter 9

▶ **minimum wage**

　最低賃金。雇用者が労働者に対して、最低限支払わなければならない賃金の下限額のこと。金額については、最低賃金法に基づき国が定めている。日本国内では、都道府県ごとに定められたもの（地域別最低賃金）と、特定の産業に対して地域別最低賃金よりも高い金額を設定したもの（特定最低賃金）の2種類がある。

▶ **living wage**

　生活賃金。労働者とその家族の一定水準の生活を保障すべきだという考えに基づき算出された賃金のこと。

　イギリスでは生活賃金の概念が広く浸透しており、労働組合や宗教団体などによって組織された団体が、毎年各地域ごとの物価等を考慮した上で生活賃金の額を決定し、企業や雇用者に対して採用するよう働きかけている。（2016年時点での生活賃金は、ロンドンで時給9.40ポンド、他の地域では時給8.25ポンドであった。）法令ではないため遵守義務はないが、2016年時点で、英国全土の約2,500の雇用者がこの生活賃金を採用している。

　一方、遵守義務がある最低賃金制度として、「全国生活賃金」が2016年4月から英国内で開始された。名称は前段の生活賃金と似ているものの、生活水準等は考慮されておらず、一般的な生活賃金の概念とは異なるものである。2016年時点での金額を、前段の遵守義務のない生活賃金と比べると、ロンドンでは約24%、それ以外の地域では約13%低い水準（時給7.20ポンド（25歳以上））となっている。

Chapter 10

▶ **Makoko**

　マココ。ナイジェリアの最大都市ラゴスにある水上スラム街。ラゴスは超高層ビルが立ち並び教育水準も高いアフリカ有数の大都市であるが、一方でそこには大規模なスラム街も多く存在する。マココは本文では island of Makoko となっているが島ではない。もともとは地元漁師の集まる集落だったが、街の発展から取り残された貧しい人々が集まるスラム街になった。10万人以上の人々が水上の粗末な家で暮らしている。

▶ **Nigeria**

　ナイジェリア。正式名称はナイジェリア連邦共和国（Federal Republic of Nigeria）。アフリカ西部に位置する国で、産油量は世界第7位である。BRICs（Brazil, Russia, India, China の4か国の頭文字から名付けられた）に次いで経済成長が期待される NEXT11（新興国経済発展国家群）の1つに数えられている。IMFによると、2010年～2012年のナイジェリアの実質GDP成長率は平均して7.3%で、同時期の世界の実質GDP平均成長率3.2%の2倍以上である。しかし長年の軍事独裁政権によって原油収入が適切に利用されておらず、貧困の緩和やインフラの整備は進んでいない。

▶ **brand-name goods**

　ブランド商品。ブランドとは、自社の製品、サービスを他社のものと区別するための名称やシンボルマーク、デザイン、あるいはそれらを組み合わせたもののことである。本文に登場する「ブランド商品」は「有名（大手）企業の商品」という意味であり、「高級ブランド商品」という意味ではない。

▶ Sub-Saharan Africa

サブサハラアフリカ。アフリカ大陸のサハラ砂漠以南を指し、略称はサブサハラ。その経済は2000年代では高成長を持続しており、それを牽引するのが豊富な資源をもつ南アフリカとナイジェリアである。高成長の要因としては、2000年代初めにかけてサブサハラにおける内戦の沈静化や民主化の進展、中国やインドなど新興国の成長にともなう資源輸出量の増大、民間消費の拡大が挙げられる。

▶ Kenya

ケニア。正式名称はケニア共和国（Republic of Kenya）。比較的工業化が進んでいるものの、コーヒー、茶、園芸作物などの農産物生産を中心とする農業国。労働力人口の約60%が農業従事者である。

▶ Nestle

ネスレ社。1866年に設立された、コーヒー関連製品を中心に食品・ペットケア商品などを製造販売する企業。コーヒー製品が有名だが、設立当初は母乳で育つことができない新生児のためのベビーフードの開発を行っていた。同社の代表的な商品「ネスカフェ」は世界180カ国以上で毎秒5,500杯以上飲まれている。2010年の同社の売上高はアフリカだけで約2,880億円で、前年より6.4%増加している。

▶ world's poorest countries

世界銀行は、1日1.25ドル未満で暮らす人々の比率を「国際貧困ライン」と定義している。2005年の時点で途上国全体では4人に1人、サブサハラにおいては2人に1人の割合で絶対的貧困層が存在する。

また、世界銀行は、国民の豊かさや貧困はその国のGDP（国内総生産）と必ずしも相関関係にあるわけではなく、政府による分配が適切に行われているかが問題だと考えている。例えば、軍事費などの予算が優先され、社会保障や教育などに分配されなければ、国民は貧しい生活を強いられることになる。そのような状態を数値で表すのが、国連開発計画（United development Programme）が発表している HDI（Human Development Index：人間開発指数）である。HDI は平均余命、成人識字指数などから計算され、0から1の間で示される。毎年発表されるランキングの下位10か国は、この数年の間すべてサブサハラの国々である。

Chapter 11

▸ reef

礁。航海に支障があるような浅い海底の高まりのこと。岩礁（岩石による高まり）とサンゴ礁がある。

▸ coral reef

サンゴ礁。サンゴは、イソギンチャクと同じ刺胞動物の一種で、分裂を繰り返して群体を作るという特性がある。サンゴ礁とは、分裂を繰り返したサンゴが積み重なって海面近くまで高まった地形を指す名称である。

サンゴ礁を形成する造礁サンゴは、海深 50m 以下で海水温 18 〜 35℃、塩分濃度 3 〜 4% の海域で成育する。サンゴは約 800 種類あり、それらの外見はそれぞれ大きく異なり、一様ではない。造礁サンゴは、海中のプランクトンを捕食する他、その体内に光合成を行う多数の植物（褐虫藻）を内包していて、そこからエネルギーを得ている。海水温の上昇や海水の汚染などによって褐虫藻が死滅すると、石灰質でできているサンゴの白色が目立つようになり、やがてサンゴは死滅（白化）する。

▸ sponge

海綿動物。最も原始的な多細胞動物だとされている。基本的には壺型の形状で、上端に口が開き、中央に胃腔がある。

Chapter 12

▸ lizard

トカゲ。有鱗目トカゲ亜目に分類される爬虫類の総称。南極以外のすべての大陸に生息し、様々な環境に適応している。昆虫や果実など想像に難くないものから、魚介類や鳥類に至るまで、その食性も様々である。日本国内でよく見られる種類として、ニホントカゲ、ニホンカナベビ、ニホンヤモリなどが挙げられる。

▸ New Guinea

ニューギニア島。太平洋南部に位置し、現在では島の東半分をパプアニューギニアが、西半分をインドネシアが領有している。面積は日本のおよそ 2 倍で、熱帯気候に属する。世界で 3 番目に大きい熱帯雨林を有し、世界の生物種全体のうち 8% が生息すると言われている。

▸ bile

胆汁。肝臓で生成されるアルカリ性の黄褐色の液体で、人間では 1 日に 600ml 〜 1L ほど分泌される。消化酵素は含まないが、脂肪の消化吸収を助ける役割がある。黄褐色の元となる色素はビリルビンと呼ばれるもので、赤血球のヘモグロビンが分解されて作られる。生成された胆汁は一時的に胆のうに貯えられ、濃色された後、消化の際に十二指腸へと送られる。

▸ *Science Advances*

『サイエンス・アドバンシズ』。世界的に権威のある学術雑誌、『サイエンス』誌を発行するアメリカ科学振興協会（American Association for the Advancement of Science）が 2015 年より発行を始めたオンライン学術誌。生命科学、物理科学、社会科学、コンピュータ科学、環境科学など幅広い分野をカバーしており、『サイエンス』誌同様に厳しい査読を通過した、質の高い最新記事を随時公開している。

▸ Christopher Austin

クリストファー・オースティン。ルイジアナ州立大学で、は虫両生類学の准教授を務める生物学者。分子遺伝学（生物が進化する過程で変化する DNA を観察し、遺伝現象を分子レベルから解明しようとする学問）の手法を用いて、は虫類や両生類の生態や進化について、ニューギニア島を中心に調査活動を行っている。

▶ **paradise kingfisher**

ラケットカワセミ。ニューギニアやモルッカ諸島の熱帯または亜熱帯気候の湿った低地林に生息する、9種のラケットカワセミの総称。共通の特徴として、赤いくちばしとカラフルな羽が挙げられる。

シラオラケットカワセミ

▶ **malaria**

マラリア。病原体となるマラリア原虫が寄生するハマダラカに刺されることで発症する病気。アジア、アフリカ、オセアニア、中東、中南米などの熱帯、亜熱帯気候の広い地域で流行している。WHO（世界保健機関）の統計によれば、全世界で年間約2億人が発症し、およそ45万人が死亡している。潜伏期間は1週間から1ヵ月とされ、発症すると高熱、頭痛、嘔吐などの症状に襲われる。処置を怠れば重症化するが、迅速に対応することで治療が可能。殺虫剤や専用の蚊よけスプレー、予防薬の内服などによる予防が有効とされている。

▶ **Michael Ollerman**

マイケル・エーラーマン。タスマニア大学に所属する特別博士研究員。海洋生物学、海洋科学を専門とする。

Chapter 13

▶ New World

新世界。大航海時代、ヨーロッパ人が発見した大陸（北米・南米大陸）やオセアニア地域を指す。これに対して、既知のヨーロッパ、アジア、アフリカは old world「旧世界」である。

▶ Industrial Revolution

産業革命。18世紀中ごろから19世紀にイギリスで起こった工場制機械工業の革命的な発達のこと。蒸気機関の改良や新技術の開発によって、それまでの手工業中心の生産から機械による大量生産へと移行していった。

産業革命は社会構成にも大きな影響を与えた。社会的な階級は、

1）地代などの財産所得に依存する地主
2）経営者として利潤を追求する資本家
3）賃金で雇われる労働者

の3つに分かれた。やがて資本主義化された社会の広まりとともに、貴族階級は失権した。現代資本主義社会の基本的な形は、この時に誕生したと言える。

1763年、7年戦争後の Treaty of Paris「パリ条約」により、フランスからカナダ・ルイジアナ東部の植民地を得て、イギリスは巨大な資源と市場を手に入れた。また、農法の改革によって食料の増産が可能になり（農業革命）、人口が増加し（人口革命）、労働人口を確保できるようになった。

1785年、James Watt「ジェームズ・ワット」によって蒸気機関が改良され、主産業である綿産業に用いる織機、紡績機の性能が向上し、綿布の著しい増産に寄与した。蒸気船や蒸気機関車が開発されて、輸送効率が上がり（交通革命）、豊富にあった石炭からコークス燃料を作る技術も開発され（エネルギー革命）、製鉄技術が向上した。以上のように、農法改革、人口増加、蒸気機関による工業力の向上が相まって、産業革命が推進された。

技術力、経済力を得た市民が力を持つようになり、医師や法律家などの専門職の地位が向上するという社会構造の変化も、産業革命の産物である。

▶ population growth ...

16〜17世紀におけるフランスの人口増加率は、年平均0.1%以下で推移していた。一組の夫婦が4〜5人の子どもを生んでも、成人に達するのは2〜3人だったため、人口の増加は限定的であった。

それまでは、衛生の悪さや凶作、疫病の流行、戦争などにより大量の死者が発生していたが、1740年から43年の飢饉と疫病を最後に、大量死は発生しなくなった。このことは、産業革命にも一因があると考えられている。

西欧主要都市の人口推移（単位：千人）

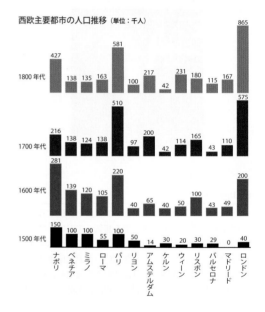

▶ French Revolution

　フランス革命。財政悪化、王室による無駄遣い、不公正税制、凶作による経済危機などにより、1789年に起きた市民革命。人権宣言により、アンシャン・レジーム（旧体制）は完全に否定され、王政は消滅した。1799年、混乱の中で登場したナポレオンの軍事クーデターにより、革命は終わった。

　アメリカ独立戦争が勃発すると、フランスはアメリカと同盟を結んで参戦する。戦争には勝利したが、国家財政は著しく悪化した。1789年、国王ルイ16世は、聖職者（第一身分）、貴族（第二身分）、市民と農民（第三身分）を召集し、三部会を開催して、第一、第二身分からも新たに税を徴収しようとした（それ以前は免税特権があった）。彼らは徴税されることに反対し、従来通り第三身分だけに課税するよう主張した。しかし、第三身分の富裕層と経済的に繋がっていた一部の貴族が、新たな議会を作り主導権を握った。主導権を譲りたくない王室は、この議会を解散させるために軍を動員した。折からの凶作もあいまって民衆の怒りは爆発し、圧政の象徴であるバスチーユ牢獄を襲撃して、フランス革命が始まった。

　数度のクーデターや政権の交代を重ねる間に、国王ルイ16世と王妃マリー・アントワネットは処刑された。1799年にナポレオンが登場し、彼の軍事クーデターによる政権奪取によって、革命は終わった。

アンシャン・レジームの風刺画

第三身分（市民、農民）が、第一身分（聖職者）と第二身分（貴族）を背負っている。

▶ unfair tax system

　不公正税制。フランス革命以前、聖職者（第一身分、約14万人）と貴族（第二身分、約40万人）は、フランス国土の4割を領有し、数多くの特権を握っていた。中でも最大の特権は免税特権だった。

　国家財政がひっ迫する中で、市民と農民（第三身分、約2,500万人）に対する度重なる増税が行われた。個人への課税率に決まったルールはなく、恣意的に決められていたらしい。収益に対して8割の税率を課されたケースもあったと言われている。

Chapter 14

▶ the Titanic

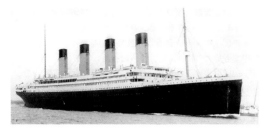

　タイタニック号。正式名称「RMS Titanic」。RMSは「Royal Mail Ship」の略で、郵便物を輸送する郵便船であった。同時に全長 269.1m、全幅 28.2m、全高 53m、乗客定員 1324 人、乗組員 899 人という、当時では世界最大級の大きさを誇る豪華客船でもあった。1912 年 4 月 14 日に北大西洋で氷山に衝突し、翌日に沈没した。

タイタニック号の航路と沈没位置

1912 年 4 月 10 日 11:45	サウサンプトンを出航。乗客数は 2,208 人。
1912 年 4 月 14 日 23:40	大西洋上で氷山に衝突。
1912 年 4 月 15 日 02:05	最後の救命艇が出される。（1,500 人以上の乗員乗客がタイタニック号に残された）
1912 年 4 月 15 日 02:20	カナダ・ニューファンドランド島沖合 640Km、深さ 4,000m の大西洋に沈没。
1912 年 4 月 15 日 04:10	救助信号を受信した客船「カルパチア」が現地に到着。
1912 年 4 月 15 日 09:00	705 人の生存者を乗せた「カルパチア」がニューヨークに到着。
1985 年 9 月	深海探査船「アルゴ」によってタイタニックの沈没現場が判明。
2009 年 5 月 31 日	最後の生存者ミルビナ・ディーンさんが 97 歳で死去。事故当時、生後 10 週間だった彼女は、郵便物の袋に入れられ、優先的に救命艇に乗せられた。

▶ iceberg

　氷河や大陸の氷が海に流れ出した非常に固く巨大な氷の塊のこと。この氷は地上に積もった雪が長い年月をかけ氷化したもので塩分を含まず、水面上に出ているものはその体積の 10％程度である。このため水面上の部分から氷山全体の大きさや形状を推測することは難しい。

　氷山が見られるのは南氷洋と北大西洋の高緯度地域に限られている。特に北大西洋の氷山は尖った山状のものが多い。

▶ Greenland

　グリーンランド。北極海と北大西洋の間にある世界最大の島で、全島の 80％以上は氷床と万年雪に覆われている。大量の氷が存在し、地球上の真水の 7％超がグリーンランドにあると言われている。

　1721 年にデンマークの植民地になったが、1953 年にはデンマークの憲法改正により植民地支配が終わり、グリーンランドはデンマークの郡（日本では都道府県に相当）となった。その後 1979 年には自治権を獲得し、2009 年には公式にデンマーク王国の自治領となった。

グリーンランドの航空写真

Chapter 15

▶ **the moon's approach to Earth**

地球の潮の干満に影響を与えているのは月と太陽である。潮の干満を引き起こす潮汐力（ちょうせきりょく）は太陽の引力と月の引力、地球の公転による遠心力で引き起こされる。太陽は地球から距離が離れているため、その潮汐力は月の半分程度である。太陽、月、地球が一直線に並ぶ新月や満月のときは、月と太陽の潮汐力が重なり、通常よりも干満差が大きい「大潮」になる。

本文掲載の「月原因説」には反論もある。シカゴのある天文学者は、「月の近地点通過と満月と新月の重なりは数年おきに発生しており氷山流出にはあまり影響しない」「潮汐力の増大も通常の近地点通過と比べて5%程度に過ぎない」と述べている。

▶ **TV addiction**

テレビ中毒。日本の学生は、他国の学生よりもテレビの視聴時間が長いという調査結果がある。とくに中学2年生では、ほぼ8割の生徒が1日2時間以上をテレビ視聴に費やす。

テレビの平均視聴時間
（中学2年生、1日あたり）

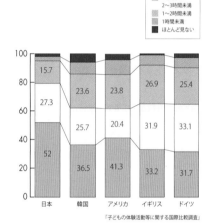

凡例：
- 3時間以上
- 2～3時間未満
- 1～2時間未満
- 1時間未満
- ほとんど見ない

「子どもの体験活動等に関する国際比較調査」

▶ **the Bible**

聖書。紀元前1450年頃から千年を超える年月の間に、多くの人によって書かれた本を1つにまとめたものである。全66巻あり、そこには律法、歴史、詩、知恵の言葉やことわざ、日記、手紙などが書かれている。

聖書は、the Old Testament「旧約聖書」と the New Testament「新約聖書」の2つの部分からできている。

旧約聖書はユダヤ教とキリスト教の聖典で、一部はイスラム教の啓典にもなっている。古代イスラエル人の何世紀にも渡る物語であり、キリスト自身も読んでいたとされる。

新約聖書はキリスト誕生後の、イエスとその最初の使徒たちの物語で、イエスの教えと、人々がイエスに導かれる様子が書かれている。現存する聖書は全て写本であり、原本は存在しない。

bible という語は、ギリシア語のビブリオンに由来する。ビブリオンとは、古代の紙の原料である papyrus「パピルス」の髄（皮をむいた内側）の部分のこと。

Chapter 16

▶ the number of road deaths

交通事故死者数。内閣府「令和2年版交通安全白書」によると近年では死者数は減少している。死者数は1970年の1万6,800人がピークであり、その死者数が日清戦争での死者数の1万7,000人と近いことから、「第一次交通戦争」と呼ぶ。これは戦後の経済成長に伴い自動車産業が発展し、車の利用が増大したのが要因とされる。また、当時の道路整備における第一の目的は輸送車が通行しやすいことだったため、歩行者の通行を考慮していない整備が行われたことも要因の1つであると考えられている。その後、交通違反の取り締まりの強化やシートベルトの義務化、法律の厳罰化、自動車の安全技術の進歩などにより、死者数が減少している。2020年の死者数は2,839人で初めて3,000人を下回り、統計開始以降最小の交通事故死者数となった。

自動車事故発生件数と死亡者数の推移

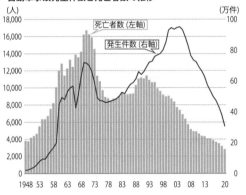

▶ self-driving car

自動運転車。人間による運転操作なしで走行できる自動車。現在、国土交通省が自動運転レベルを0〜5の6段階に分けて定義し、それぞれのレベルで運転の主体や走行領域を設定している。6段階のうち、0〜2の3レベルが人間の監視下で行われる自動運転、3〜5の3レベルが車のシステムによる自動運転とされている。現在普及している自動ブレーキや車線維持はレベル1、高速道路での自動合流や自動追い越しはレベル2となる。

自動運転システムの実験は1920年代から行われている。最初の自動運転車は1977年に筑波大学機械工学研究所によって開発された。この自動車は2つのカメラが道路上の白線を検知して走行するもので、時速32kmでの走行だった。

2018年にはアメリカ合衆国アリゾナ州で、配車サービスを提供するウーバー・テクノロジーズ社のテスト中の自動運転車による歩行者死亡事故が発生した。これは横断歩道のない場所で道路を横断していた女性を自動運転車がはねて死亡させたというものだった。この事故は乗り心地を優先して自動運転車の緊急ブレーキ機能が切られていたことが原因とされ、事故の責任の所在が議論されることとなった。最終的には配車したウーバー・テクノロジーズ社が遺族に和解金を支払うこととなった。

2021年3月4日、ホンダ社はレベル3認定の自動運転装置を搭載した自動車「レジェンド」を発売した。これは世界初のレベル3認定自動車であり、またその技術も世界初のものだった。

Chapter 17

▶ Roger Ekirch

ロジャー・イカーチ。1950年生まれ。バージニア工科大学の歴史学科教授。本文に登場する分割睡眠に関する論文は、2001年に学術誌 *The American Historical Review* に掲載された。2005年に発表された彼の著作 *At Day's Close: Night in Times Past* は、英国の高級紙 *The Observer* が発表する *An Observer Books of the Year, 2005* をはじめ多くの賞を受賞した。日本語翻訳本は2015年1月に『失われた夜の歴史』（インターシフト社）のタイトルで出版されている。

▶ coffee house

コーヒーハウス（カフェ、喫茶店）。15世紀には現在のサウジアラビアの都市であるメッカにいくつものコーヒーハウスがあった。17世紀初頭に貿易商人がコーヒー豆をヨーロッパに輸入するようになると、ロンドンやパリ、ウィーンといったヨーロッパの都市にコーヒーハウスが出現するようになった。水かアルコール以外のものを飲む習慣がほとんどなかった当時のヨーロッパの人々にとって、コーヒーは、非アルコールとしては初めて経験する「刺激的な」飲み物だった。さらに、健康によい働きがあると考えられていたため、コーヒーの人気は急速に高まった。

17世紀の一般的なコーヒーハウスは、アルコール類や料理はメニューになく、多数の新聞や雑誌が置かれ、女性の入店は禁じられていた。17世紀後半には、ロンドンのコーヒーハウスは2,000店を超えていたが、18世紀後半以降、紅茶の普及もあって急速に減少した。

ロンドンのコーヒーハウスの様子（17世紀）

▶ wax candles in glass lamps

ルイ14世の指示で街路に設置された、四角いガラス製ケースに1本のろうそくを備えた照明器具。1667年に912の街路に2,736個が設置され、18世紀後半には約8,000個が設置されていた。初期の街灯は、街路の上にロープを張り、その中央にランタン（吊り下げ式のランプ）が取り付けてられていた。現代のようにスイッチで点灯できるわけではなかったので、点灯夫（lamplighter）が数千におよぶロウソクの一つひとつに火を灯していた。

難点は、ガラスケースに囲われてはいたが風に弱く、すぐに消えてしまうことだった。満月の夜は、「月の光だけで十分明るい」という理由で点灯されないことが多かった。

17世紀のパリの街灯

▶ oil-powered lamp

オイルランプ。この当時のオイルランプの燃料は石油由来の油ではなく、動物や植物の油だった。

パリの街灯は、1760年代から動物の油を使ったオイルランプに順次切り替わっていった。オイルランプはロウソクに比べてはるかに明るいため、パリの治安は大きく改善した。それまで朝になると、市中を流れるセーヌ川には年間100体以上の身元不明者の遺体があがっていたが、その数が劇的に減少したと言われている。

Chapter 18

▶ Harvard

　ハーバード大学。創立 1636 年、米国有数の難関大学で、学生数は 19,000 人。英国高等教育専門誌 *Times Higher Education* によると、2013 年の世界大学ランキングは 4 位だった（1 位はカリフォルニア工科大学）。

　有名な卒業生は、オバマ大統領、ジョン・F・ケネディ、セオドア・ルーズベルトなど、枚挙にいとまがない。マイクロソフト社の創業者ビル・ゲイツ、フェイスブックの開発者マーク・ザッカーバーグも、本大学に通った（両者とも中退している）。

世界大学ランキング 2013

1 位	カリフォルニア工科大学（米）
2 位	スタンフォード大学（米）
3 位	オックスフォード大学（英）
4 位	ハーバード大学（米）
5 位	マサチューセッツ工科大学（米）
27 位	東京大学
54 位	京都大学
128 位	東京工業大学
137 位	東北大学
147 位	大阪大学

Source: *The Times Higher Education*

▶ the Gallup Poll

　ギャラップ調査。アメリカの心理学者・統計学者の George H. Gallup「ジョージ・ギャラップ（1901-1984）」は、新聞の世論調査の重要性を認識し、1935 年に American Institute of Public Opinion を設立した。今日の標本調査では常識となった random sampling「無作為抽出法」を定着させた。1935 年以来毎週、政治、経済、社会などのジャンルについて世論調査を行い、その結果は 150 の新聞に掲載されている。

Cutting Edge
Green

定価 700 円＋税

初刷発行：2024 年 10 月 25 日

編著者：山本一太

株式会社 エミル出版

〒102-0072 東京都千代田区飯田橋 2-8-1
TEL 03-6272-5481　FAX 03-6272-5482
ISBN978-4-86449-156-3 C7082

Cutting Edge

Green

Navi Book

Chapter 1: Recently, ...

Chapter 2: Have you ever heard ...

Chapter 10: Born and raised on ...

Chapter 11: Since antient times, ...

Chapter 11: Most people know ...

Chapter 11: The number of ...

ÉMILE

◆ 【語句】

　意味が空欄になっているものは、すべて入試必出の「重要語句」です。分からなければ辞書を引いて、覚えるまで何度も確認しましょう。

◆ 【本文解説 & Check Drill】

　入試頻出の、少し分かりにくい構文、文構造を解説しています。難しいと感じた文については、問題を全て解いたあとでこの解説を読んで確認しましょう。また、参考書や辞書で検索しやすいように見出しをつけていますので、理解できるまで、自分で調べることが大切です。この「じっくりと読んで理解する」作業を怠ると、学習効果は半減します。粘り強く繰り返すことで、知らず知らずのうちに「読める」ようになるのです。解説が理解できたら Check Drill を解き、理解度を確認しましょう。

◆ 【段落要旨・百字要約】

　各段落ごとの要旨を完成させて、百字要約につなげる演習をします。この演習を繰り返すことで、国公立大の二次試験で問われる「要約力」「記述力」を効率的に養うことができます。

　やみくもに「書く」ことを繰り返しても、要約する力は身につきません。要約文を完成させるためには、「必要な情報と不必要な情報の選別」と「必要な情報をつなぎ合わせること」に慣れる必要があります。ここではその2点を意識しながら演習できるように構成されています。

● 目次 ●

Recently, researchers from the Union of Concerned Scientists in the U.S. released a report on how consumer behavior affects the environment. Their study showed that meat consumption is one of the main ways that humans can damage the environment, second only to the use of motor vehicles.

So, how can a simple thing like eating meat have a negative effect on the environment? The most important impact of meat production is through the use of water and land. Two thousand five hundred gallons of water are needed to produce one pound of beef, whereas only twenty gallons of water are needed to produce one pound of wheat.

(1)By producing crops instead of animals, we can make more efficient use of the land and water. One acre of farmland that is used for raising livestock can produce 250 pounds of beef. One acre of farmland used for crops can produce 40,000 pounds of potatoes, 30,000 pounds of carrots, or 50,000 pounds of tomatoes.

Furthermore, (2)farm animals add to the problem of global warming. All livestock animals such as cows, pigs, and sheep release methane* by expelling gas from their bodies. One cow can produce up to sixty liters of methane each day. Methane gas is the second most common greenhouse gas after carbon dioxide. Many environmental experts now believe that methane is more responsible for global warming than carbon dioxide. It is estimated that twenty-five percent of all methane released into the atmosphere comes from farm animals.

People are becoming aware of the benefits of switching to a vegetarian diet, not just for health reasons, but also because it plays a vital role in protecting the environment. (3)Some people go further, and eat a vegan diet, which excludes all products from animal sources, such as cheese, eggs, and milk. However, some nutritionists believe that a vegan diet can be deficient in some of the vitamins and minerals that our bodies need daily.

Today, many people are concerned about improving their health, and about protecting the environment. Switching to a vegetarian diet — or just eating less meat — is a good way to do both of these things at the same time.

＊ methane「メタンガス」

1

2

3

4

5

語句　音声は、「英語」→「日本語の意味」の順で読まれます。　CD 1 - Tr 7 〜 10

入試基本レベル

2	behavior [bihéivjər]	
2	affect [əfékt]（動）	
3	damage [dǽmidʒ]（動）	
5	effect on 〜	
6	impact [ímpækt]（名）	
6	production [prədʌ́kʃən]	
7	produce [prəd(j)úːs]（動）	
10	crop [krάp]	
10	instead of 〜	
18	be responsible for 〜	
20	atmosphere [ǽtməsfìər]	
21	benefit [bénəfit]（名）	
22	play a role in 〜	
22	protect [prətékt]	
27	be concerned about 〜	
27	improve [imprúːv]	

入試標準レベル（共通テスト・私大）

1	concerned [kənsə́rnd]	
2	consumer [kənsúːmər]	
3	consumption [kənsʌ́mpʃən]	
4	vehicle [víːhikl]	
8	whereas [hweərǽz]	
9	wheat [hwíːt]	
10	make use of 〜	

10	efficient [ifíʃənt]	
11	farmland [fάːrmlænd]	
14	furthermore [fə́ːrðərmɔ̀ːr]	
16	up to 〜	
17	greenhouse gas	
17	carbon dioxide	
19	estimate [éstəmèit]（動）	
21	be aware of 〜	
22	vital [váitl]	
24	source [sɔ́ːrs]（名）	

入試発展レベル（二次・有名私大）

11	livestock [láivstὰk]	家畜
15	expel [ekspél]	〜を（吐き）出す
21	switch to 〜	〜に切り替える
23	exclude [eksklúːd]	〜を除外する
25	nutritionist [n(j)u(ː)tríʃənist]	栄養学者
25	be deficient in 〜	〜が不足している

その他

4	second only to 〜	〜に次いで 2 番目の
7	gallon [gǽlən]	ガロン
8	pound [páund]	ポンド
11	acre [éikər]	エーカー
21	vegetarian diet	菜食
23	vegan diet	完全菜食主義の食事

3

1 【名詞節を導く疑問詞】（第1段落第1文）

Recently, researchers from the Union of Concerned Scientists in the U.S. released a report on **how** consumer behavior affects the environment.

▶ 疑問詞が導く節は、名詞節として主語、補語、目的語などの働きをする。上の例は how 以下が前置詞 on の目的語になっている。

2 【the way ＋ (that / in which) ＋ S ＋ V】（第1段落第2文）

… meat consumption is one of **the main ways that** humans can damage the environment …

▶ the way を先行詞として関係詞節を続ける場合、関係副詞 how を用いることができない。一般的には how を省略して〈the way S ＋ V〉とすることが多いが、the way in which … や、この文のように the way that … と表現されることもある。この場合の that は関係副詞である。

3 【not only A but also B】（第5段落第1文）

People are becoming aware of the benefits of switching to a vegetarian diet, **not just** for health reasons, **but also** because it plays a vital role in protecting the environment.

▶ not only A but also B は「A だけでなく B も」を意味する頻出表現。A と B は文中での文法的働きが同じものになる。上の例は A が for health reasons という副詞句、B が because 以下の副詞節になっている。また、本例のように、only の代わりに just、simply、merely などが用いられることもあり、but also の also は省略されることもある。

Check Drill　1、2は語句を並べ替え、3〜5は日本語に訳しなさい。

1.　人が私の服装をどう思おうが気にしません。　(昭和大)

I don't care (people / the way / other / dress / think / what / of / I).

2.　タンパク質は人間にとってだけでなく、魚にとっても重要なエネルギー源です。　(名城大・改)

Protein is an important energy (human / only / source / fish / beings / but / not / for / for) as well.

3.　How he got over the difficulty is a mystery to us.　(国士舘大・改)

4.　Calculate what percentage of your income you spend on food.　(自治医科大・改)

5.　The way he laughs reminds me of his father very much.　(明治学院大・改)

展開	段落	要旨
導入	1	人間による（①　　　　　）の消費が環境に被害を与える、と発表された。
本論①	2	（①　　　　　）を生産するときの（②　　　　　）と土地の利用が、環境に大きな影響を与える。
本論②	3	（③　　　　　）を生産すれば、家畜を育てる以上に（②　　　　）や土地を有効利用できる。
本論③	4	さらに、家畜は温室効果ガスの１つである（④　　　　　　）を放出し、 （⑤　　　　　　　）を深刻化させている。
本論④	5	（⑥　　　　　　　）や環境保護の観点から、人々は菜食に切り替える利点を意識しつつある。
結論	6	菜食にすることや食べる肉を減らすことは、（⑥　　　　　　）と環境保護の両方にとって有益である。

■　以下を参考にして、「段落要旨」の下線部分を中心にまとめてみよう。
　▶「導入」の内容（20 ～ 25 字）
　▶「本論①～③」の内容（55 ～ 65 字）
　「本論」の内容は「導入（＝主題）」の詳しい説明になっているので、「導入」に対する〈理由〉や〈根拠〉を
　表すようにまとめると、自然なつながりになる。　【記述例】：「～の生産は…だからだ」
　▶「結論」の内容（20 ～ 25 字）

（下書き）

CD 1

How much water do you think an ordinary person really needs to drink per day? ✎11 Many people believe they are supposed to drink eight glasses of water a day, or about two liters. Why? Because that is what they have been told all their lives. But a recent report offers some different advice. Experts say people should obey their bodies; they should drink as much water as they feel like drinking.

The report says most healthy people meet their daily needs for liquid by (1)letting ✎12 thirst be their guide. The report is from the Institute of Medicine, part of the American National Academies. This organization provides scientific and technical advice to the government and the public. The report contains some general suggestions. The experts say women should get about 2.7 liters of water daily. Men should get about 3.7 liters. But wait — in each case, those are more than eight glasses. There is one important difference. The report does not tell people how many glasses of water to drink. In fact, the experts say it may be impossible to know how many glasses are needed to meet these guidelines. This is because the daily water requirement can include the water content in foods.

(2)People do not get water only by forcing themselves to drink a set number of ✎13 glasses of it per day. People also drink fruit juices and sodas or milk. Of course they may also drink coffee and tea. These all contain water. Yet some also contain caffeine. This causes the body to get rid of more water. But the writers of the report say this does not mean the body loses too much water. As you might expect, the Institute of Medicine says people usually need to drink more water when they are physically active. (3)The same is true of those who live in hot climates. Depending on heat and activity, some people could drink two times as much water as others do.

All this, however, does not answer one question. No one seems sure why people ✎14 have the idea that good health requires eight glasses of water daily. It may have started with (4)a misunderstanding. In 1945, the American National Academy of Sciences published (5)some guidelines. Its Food and Nutrition Board* said a good amount of water for most adults was 2.5 liters daily. This was based on an average of one milliliter for each kilocalorie of food eaten. But that was only part of what the board said. It also said that most of this amount is contained in prepared foods.

* Food and Nutrition Board「食品栄養部会」

❶ ....

❷ ....
....

❸ ....

❹ 公表された1日に必要な水分量の大半は [　][　][　][　][　][　][　][　][　][　][　][　] [　][　][　][　] いたが、その水分量を [　][　][　][　][　][　][　][　][　][　][　][　] [　][　][　][　] だと誤解したこと。

❺ ....liters

❻ ....

語句　音声は、「英語」→「日本語の意味」の順で読まれます。　CD 1 - Tr 15 〜 18

入試基本レベル

2	*be* supposed to *do*	....
4	offer [ɔ́(ː)fər]	....
5	feel like *doing*	....
6	let O *do*	....
7	guide [gáid]（名）	....
7	medicine [médəsn]	医学
8	organization [ɔ̀ːrgənəzéiʃən]	....
8	provide [prəváid]	....
9	public [pʌ́blik]	〔the 〜で〕一般大衆
9	contain [kəntéin]	....
9	general [dʒénərəl]	....
10	suggestion [sə(g)dʒéstʃən]	....
15	requirement [rikwáiərmənt]	....
15	include [inklúːd]	....
16	force O to *do*	....
19	cause O to *do*	....
19	get rid of 〜	....
20	expect [ekspékt]	....
22	climate [kláimət]	....
22	depending on 〜	....
25	require [rikwáiər]	....
27	publish [pʌ́bliʃ]	....
28	*be* based on 〜	....

28	average [ǽvəridʒ]	....

入試標準レベル（共通テスト・私大）

1	ordinary [ɔ́ːrdənèri]	....
4	obey [oubéi]	....
6	liquid [líkwid]	....
7	institute [ínstətùːt]（名）	....
14	meet [míːt]	....
14	guideline [gáidlàin]	....
15	content [kántent]（名）	....
21	physically [fízikəli]	....
22	*be* true of 〜	....
26	misunderstanding [mìsʌ̀ndərstǽndiŋ]	....
27	a good amount of 〜	....

入試発展レベル（二次・有名私大）

1	per 〜	〜当たり
7	thirst [θə́ːrst]	のどの渇き
16	set [sét]（形）	定められた、規定の

その他

30	prepared [pripéərd]	調理された

1 【関係代名詞 what】（第 1 段落第 4 文）

Because that is **what** they have been told all their lives.

▶ この what は関係代名詞で、名詞節を導いている。関係代名詞の what は、他の関係代名詞と違って先行詞がない。what 自身に先行詞 the thing が含まれていて、what = the thing which と考えるとわかりやすい。意味は、先行詞 the thing の意味も含めた「～であるところのもの［こと］」になる。

2 【疑問詞＋ to *do*】（第 2 段落第 9 文）

The report does not tell people **how** many glasses of water **to drink**.

▶ 〈疑問詞＋ to *do*〉は文の主語や補語、目的語になる名詞句を作る用法で、基本的な意味は「何を［いつ］［どこで］［どのように］～すべきか［したらよいのか］」。ここでは、how many glasses of water to drink が tell の直接目的語になっている。

3 【倍数表現】（第 3 段落第 10 文）

Depending on heat and activity, some people could drink **two times as** much water **as** others do.

▶ 〈... times as ～ as ―〉で「―よりも…倍～の」を表す。「2 倍」を表す場合はこの文のように two times を使うこともあるが、一般的には〈twice as ～ as ―〉で表現される。「半分」の場合は〈half as ～ as ―〉。

Check Drill　　1～3 は語句を並べ替え、4、5 は空所に適切なものを入れて日本語に訳しなさい。

1. これは私が彼の妹から聞いたことです。　　　　　　　　　　　　　　　　　　　　（大阪産業大）

This (is / what / sister / I / from / his / heard).

2. どのバスに乗ればいいか教えてくれませんか？　　　　　　　　　　　　　　　（流通経済大・改）

(tell / bus / will / you / me / take / which / to)?

3. 私の友人はバスケットボールがとても上手だが、彼は私の 3 倍練習している。　　（センター試験）

My friend, who can play basketball very well, practices (as / as often / do / I / three times).

4. (　　　　) has not yet been decided.　　　　　　　　　　　　　　　　　　　　（浜松大）

① To go where　　② Where to go　　③ Go to where　　④ Where go to

5. Thank you, Hiromi. This book is exactly (　　　　) I wanted.　　　　　（センター試験）

① what　　② which　　③ of which　　④ that

展開	段落	要旨
導入	1	多くの人が1日に（①　　　　　　　　　　）の水を飲む必要があると信じている。だが最近では、「飲みたいだけ飲むべきだ」という主張がある。
本論①	2	報告書によれば、（②　　　　　　　　　　）を目安にするだけで1日の必要量を満たせる。それは、1日の必要水分量には（③　　　　　　　　）の水分含有量が含まれているからだ。
本論②	3	人々は水だけでなく、様々な（④　　　　　　　）からも水分を摂取する。さらに、暑さや（⑤　　　　　　）によって、必要水分量が増える。
本論③	4	1日に（①　　　　　　　　　）の水を飲む必要があるという考えは、過去の指針への（⑥　　　　　　）が発端かもしれない。その指針は、適量は1日2.5リットルだと示していた。だが、その水分量の大半は（③　　　　　　　）に含まれているという説明もしていたのだ。

■　以下を参考にして、「段落要旨」の下線部分を中心にまとめてみよう。

▶「導入」の内容（50～55字）【記述例】：「～だと専門家は言うが、…だと信じている人々が多い」

▶「本論③」前半の内容（25～30字）【記述例】：「それは～が発端だろう」

▶「本論③」後半の内容（20～25字）【記述例】：「その水分量には～が含まれていた」

（下書き）

10　　　　　　　　　　　　　　　　20

10　　　　　　　　　　　　　　　　20

One interesting thing about languages is the way they change over time. In 19 English, everything from spelling to vocabulary to pronunciation has gone through major changes over centuries. (1)In fact, to a modern speaker, the English of 1,000 years ago is like a foreign language!

5   The history of English dates back around 1,500 years. At that time, groups of 20 Europeans invaded England, bringing their languages with them. These gradually developed into Old English. Later, in 1066, England was invaded by the Normans, from France. This caused the language to go through an important shift, leading to what we now call Middle English. Over the next 500 years, the language underwent 10 further shifts, eventually evolving into Modern English. As the language has developed down to the present day, many things about it have changed.

Pronunciation is one of the most obvious areas of change. For example, in Old 21 English, people said "hus" and "mus." Now we say "house" and "mouse." These days, there are also many differences in the way English is pronounced in the USA, 15 the UK, Australia, and elsewhere. (2)When people who speak the same language live in places separated by great distances, the language undergoes rapid changes in each place.

Spelling has also gone through interesting changes. For example, in Old English, 22 people wrote "riht." A "g" was added in Middle English, making the spelling "right." 20 Also, in the distant past, people did not always follow standards of spelling. In the 18th and 19th centuries, scholars like Noah Webster wrote dictionaries which made English spelling more consistent. But different standards were decided on in England and the USA, so some differences remain — for example, "color" vs. "colour."

(3)Vocabulary changes happen even more quickly. English has grown by 23 25 borrowing words from languages such as French, Spanish, and Arabic, to name a few. This often happens with food. "Tofu" and "sushi" are now standard English words, for example, and even "edamame" is listed in some dictionaries. (4)Then there is slang, with new terms entering and leaving the language every year. Thirty years ago, you often heard people saying "groovy," meaning "great." These days, you 30 rarely hear the word, except in old movies and on old TV shows.

Because English is spoken by so many people worldwide, it really is (5)an exciting 24 time for the language. Just as American and British versions are always changing, so are versions spoken in Canada, Singapore, India, and elsewhere. At the same time, an entire new version of English is appearing on the Internet, with whole new 35 slang expressions and writing styles. So in a way, learning English is a never-ending process, even for native speakers!

1

2

3

4

5

6

語句 音声は、「英語」→「日本語の意味」の順で読まれます。　　　　　CD 1 - Tr 25 〜 28

入試基本レベル

2　**vocabulary** [vo(u)kǽbjəlèri]

2　**go through**

3　**major** [méidʒər]

6　**European** [jùərəpíːən]

6　**gradually** [grǽdʒuəli]

8　**cause 〜 to** *do*

10　**further** [fə́ːrðər]（形）

10　**eventually** [ivéntʃuəli]

12　**area** [éəriə]

16　**separate** [sépərèit]（動）

16　**distance** [dístəns]

19　**add** [ǽd]

20　**distant** [dístənt]

20　**follow** [fálou]

20　**standard** [stǽndərd]（名）

22　**decide on 〜**

23　**remain** [riméin]

25　**such as 〜**

28　**term** [tə́ːrm]

34　**appear** [əpíər]

入試標準レベル（共通テスト・私大）

1　**over time**

2　**spelling** [spéliŋ]

2　**pronunciation** [prənʌnsiéiʃən]

5　**date back**

6　**invade** [invéid]

7　**develop into 〜**

8　**shift** [ʃíft]（名）

9　**undergo** [ʌndərgóu]

10　**evolve into 〜**

11　**present** [préznt]（形）

12　**obvious** [ábviəs]

14　**pronounce** [prənáuns]

15　**elsewhere** [élshwèər]

16　**rapid** [rǽpid]

21　**scholar** [skálər]

22　**consistent** [kənsístənt]

27　**list** [líst]（動）

32　**version** [və́ːrʒən]

34　**entire** [entáiər]

35　**expression** [ekspréʃən]

35　**in a way**

入試発展レベル（二次・有名私大）

25　**to name a few**　　　いくつか例を挙げるなら

28　**slang** [slǽŋ]　　　スラング、俗語

その他

7　**Norman** [nɔ́ːrmən]　　　ノルマン人

本文解説 & Check Drill

1 【無生物主語の構文】(第2段落第5文)

This caused the language to go through an important shift, ...

▶ 「無生物主語の構文」とは、主語が「原因」、動詞の後にくる部分が「結果」を表す構文のことである。上の例は〈cause +目的語+ to +動詞の原形〉「～に…させる、～が…する原因となる」の構文だが、他に make などの第5文型をとる動詞がよく用いられる。

2 【前置詞＋動名詞】(第5段落第1文)

Vocabulary changes happen even more quickly. English has grown **by borrowing** words from languages ...

▶ 動名詞は、主語や補語、動詞の目的語の働きをするが、前置詞の目的語になる重要な用法がある。上の例の〈by +動名詞〉は「～することによって」という「手段」を表している。

3 【様態の接続詞 as】(第6段落第2文)

Just as American and British versions are always changing, **so** are versions spoken in Canada, Singapore, India, and elsewhere.

▶ 接続詞 as には様々な用法があるが、「～のように、～と同じように」という意味になる「様態」の as も重要である。上の例のように、just を伴って「ちょうど～のように」となることも多い。さらに、本例のように主節の前に so が置かれる場合もあり、so の後の語順は〈動詞＋主語〉と倒置される。

Check Drill 1～3は語句を並べ替え、4、5は空所に適切なものを入れて日本語に訳しなさい。

1. スーザンが言った言葉で、父親はひどく怒った。 (中央大・改)

   What (made / very angry / said / Susan / her father).

   ....

2. ニュートンは、なぜリンゴは地面に落ちるのかと思った。 (中央大・改)

   Newton wondered (the apple / caused / fall / what / to) to the ground.

   ....

3. その若い男は、その女性に対し、コーヒーを洋服にこぼしたことをわびた。 (共立女子大・改)

   The young man apologized (for / to / on / spilling / coffee / the woman) her dress.

   ....

4. (   ) entering the classroom, I asked my friend what was going on. (立命館大)

   ① At   ② For   ③ In   ④ On

   ....

5. Although I really like Jennifer, I don't understand why she behaves (   ) she does. (南山大)

   ① as   ② such   ③ so   ④ though

   ....

展開	段落	要旨
導入①	1	(①　　　　　)の面白さの１つは時と共に変化することだ。英語も、つづりや語い、発音などすべてが、数世紀の間に大きく変化した。
導入②	2	英語の(②　　　　　)は約 1,500 年前にさかのぼる。古英語から近代英語へと発展する中で多くのことが変化した。
具体例①	3	変化が最も明らかなのは発音だ。時代による違いだけでなく、今では、住んでいる(③　　　　　)による違いも多くある。
具体例②	4	つづりも興味深い変化を経た。18 世紀以降の(④　　　　　)の作成を通じて、より一貫性があるものになった。
具体例③	5	語いはさらに急速に変化している。英語は、他の言語から単語を(⑤　　　　　)ことで豊かになってきた。
具体例④	6	英語は世界中で非常に多くの人々に話されているため、各地域の英語も変化している。同時に(⑥　　　　　)では、表現や書き方が新しい英語が出現している。

百字要約　「段落要旨」を参考にして、本文全体の内容を百字程度の日本語で要約しなさい。

■　以下を参考にして、「段落要旨」の下線部分を中心にまとめてみよう。
　▶「導入①」の内容（40 ～ 50 字）
　▶「具体例④」の内容（50 ～ 60 字）

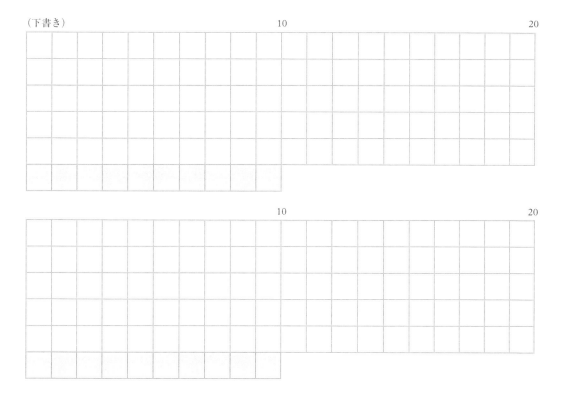

Some rich people are planning to upload their brains onto computers after they die, hoping that science will progress enough to make artificial intelligence possible. If you think this sounds like science fiction, take a look at the work of Martine Rothblatt, America's highest paid female CEO★ and founder of GeoStar, a GPS★ navigation company. Rothblatt also started Sirius Satellite Radio, a service allowing customers to hear nearly a thousand different radio stations online. In 2007 she created a simple copy of her partner's brain and uploaded it into a life-like robot known as (1)Bina48. That robot is able to have short ordinary conversations with humans. However, Bina48 is not yet able to sustain long conversations in ways that seem fully "human."

Rothblatt believes that within twenty years, "mind clones★" will be humanity's biggest invention. (2)The concept of cloning human brains and placing them inside robotic bodies has been described in numerous science fiction works. However, Google director Ray Kurzweil believes that our bodies may be replaced by machines within ninety years and that some people will become digitally immortal★. His 1999 book *The Age of Spiritual Machines: When Computers Exceed Human Intelligence* describes one possible future in which the boundaries between biological human intelligence and digital artificial intelligence blur★. Kurzweil mentions a possible future that seems both (3)promising and terrifying. If super intelligent transhumans★ become hundreds of times smarter, many problems such as hunger, war, and pollution could be solved. However, (4)there is no guarantee that such computer-based intelligence would act "fairly" by ordinary human standards. According to Kurzweil, during the late 21st century humans who become part of super-intelligent AI systems★ might start to regard ordinary humans as second-class citizens. At some point, ordinary people simply will not be able to keep up with the super-intelligent "transhumans." If you had the choice and could afford it, would you upload your own consciousness onto a computer? Would you like to purchase a robotic version of yourself?

★ CEO「最高経営責任者」 GPS「全地球測位システム」 clone「クローン」
immortal「不死身の」 blur「あいまいになる」 transhuman「トランスヒューマン、超人間」
AI system「人工知能システム」

1 ....

....

2 ....

....

3 ....

....

4 ....

....

5 (1) .... (2) ....

語句	音声は、「英語」→「日本語の意味」の順で読まれます。	CD 1 - Tr 31 〜 34

入試基本レベル

2	**progress** [prəgrés]（動）	
3	**take a look at ~**	
4	**female** [fíːmeil]	
7	**create** [kriéit]	
8	**conversation** [kànvərséiʃən]	
13	**describe** [diskráib]	
14	**replace** [ripléis]	
18	**mention** [ménʃən]（動）	
20	**hunger** [hʌ́ŋɡər]（名）	
20	**pollution** [pəlúːʃən]	
22	**fairly** [féərli]	
22	**standard** [stǽndərd]（名）	
24	**citizen** [sítizn]	
25	**keep up with ~**	
26	**choice** [tʃɔ́is]	
26	**afford** [əfɔ́ːrd]	

入試標準レベル（共通テスト・私大）

2	**artificial intelligence**	
4	**founder** [fáundər]	
8	**ordinary** [ɔ́ːrdənèri]	
9	**sustain** [səstéin]	

11	**humanity** [hjuːmǽnəti]	
12	**concept** [kánsept]	
13	**numerous** [núːmərəs]	
16	**spiritual** [spíritʃuəl]	
16	**exceed** [eksíːd]	
17	**boundary** [báund(ə)ri]	
17	**biological** [bàiəládʒikl]	
19	**terrifying** [térəfàiŋ]	
21	**guarantee** [ɡæ̀rəntíː]（名）	
24	**regard ~ as ...**	
27	**purchase** [pə́ːrtʃəs]（動）	
27	**version** [vɔ́ːrʒən]	

入試発展レベル（二次・有名私大）

19	**promising** [práməsiŋ]	前途有望な
24	**second-class**	二流の
27	**consciousness** [kánʃəsnəs]	意識

その他

1	**upload** [ʌploúd]	〜をアップロードする
6	**online** [ánláin]（副）	オンライン上で
7	**life-like**	本物そっくりの
15	**immortal** [imɔ́ːrtl]	不死身の、不滅の
18	**blur** [blə́ːr]（動）	あいまいになる

1 【分詞構文】（第1段落第1文）

Some rich people are planning to upload their brains onto computers after they die, **hoping** that science will progress enough to make artificial intelligence possible.

▶ 分詞構文は、2つの文を接続詞を用いずに、一方を分詞で始めることで1つの文にする構文である。

▶ 分詞構文が表す意味は「時」、「理由」などがあるが、上例のように主節の後に分詞構文が続く場合、「主節の補足説明」の意味になることが多い。

2 【同格の of】（第2段落第2文）

The concept **of** cloning human brains and placing them inside robotic bodies has been described in numerous science fiction works.

▶ 前置詞 of には「抽象的・一般的な名詞（idea, problem, possibility など）」の具体的な内容を表す用法があり、これを「同格」の用法と呼ぶ。of の後には、動名詞が続くことも多い。

▶ また、この動名詞の動作の主体を表すため、動名詞の前に意味上の主語が置かれることも多い。

3 【同格の that 節】（第2段落第7文）

However, there is no guarantee **that** such computer-based intelligence would act "fairly" by ordinary human standards.

▶ 同格の of と同じように、「抽象的・一般的な名詞」の具体的な内容を表すために、that 節が続くことがある。この that 節は「同格の名詞節」と呼ばれる。

Check Drill　1〜3は空所に適切なものを選んで入れ、4、5は語句を並べ替えなさい。

1. I always walk my dog along the beach, (　　　) the sea view.　　　　(センター試験)
　① being enjoyed　　② enjoy　　　　③ enjoying　　　　④ with enjoying

2. There is no hope that he will recover.　　　　(中京大・改)
　= There is no hope (　　　) his recovery.
　① in　　　　　　② of　　　　　③ at　　　　　　④ with

3. The news (　　　) she had passed the test delighted her parents.　　　(九州国際大・改)
　① about　　　　② of　　　　　③ that　　　　④ which

4. なぜ彼女は歌手になる考えを捨てたのだろう。　　　　(東邦大)

　Why did she (of / becoming / give / idea / up / the / a) singer?

....

5. 私たちは消費している食料の30%以上を海外から輸入しているという事実を認識しなければならない。　　(東洋大)

　We must (more than / the fact / 30% of our foods / recognize / come / that) from abroad.

....

展開	段落	要旨
ロスブラット の研究	1	裕福な人々の中には、死後に（①　　　　　　　）科学が発展すると考え、自分の（②　　　　）をコンピューターにアップロードすることを計画している人がいる。ロスブラットは、（③　　　　　　　）の（②　　　　）のコピーを、ビーナ48と呼ばれる人型ロボットにアップロードした。ビーナ48は、人間と短い（④　　　　　　　）を行うことができる。
カーツワイル の考え	2	ロスブラットは「（⑤　　　　　　　）」が人類最大の発明になると信じている。カーツワイルも、人の身体は近い将来（⑥　　　　）に換わり、デジタル的に不死身になる人間が現れると信じている。彼は著書の中で、超知的な「（⑦　　　　　　　　　　）」が様々な問題を解決すると同時に、（⑧　　　　　）の人間を二流の市民だと見なす未来像を描いている。

百字要約　　「段落要旨」を参考にして、本文全体の内容を百字程度の日本語で要約しなさい。

■　以下を参考にして、「段落要旨」の下線部分を中心にまとめてみよう。
　▶「ロスブラットの研究」は導入的な具体例であり、「カーツワイルの考え」前半の内容と近いためここでは省略。
　▶「カーツワイルの考え」前半の内容（45〜55字）
　【記述例】：「将来〜が発展すれば、人間は…になると考える人々がいる」
　▶「カーツワイルの考え」後半の内容（50〜60字）
　【言い換え例】：「〜する未来像を描いている」→「〜する可能性がある」

（下書き）　　　　　　　　　　　　　　　　　　　10　　　　　　　　　　　　　　　　　　　20

🔊 35

Have you ever heard of the "quagga"? Perhaps not, but you may have seen a zebra before. The zebra is a horse-like animal with distinctive black and white stripes covering its body. The quagga was a member of the zebra family, brownish in colour with white stripes around the neck and the front part of the body. It is often said that quaggas looked like "(1)zebras which had forgotten to put on their pajama trousers." Quaggas lived in Southern Africa, but they died out in the 19th century due to overhunting. We can now only see their wild beauty as stuffed specimens.

🔊 36

Some researchers, however, have tried to "revive" the quagga. (2)Because of its attractive stripe pattern, the quagga has gathered much attention from those interested in animal conservation. Those who would like to see the animals walk around the savannas again have conducted the Quagga Project for over thirty years in South Africa. It turns out that the quagga is genetically close to the plains zebra★. In this project, researchers have attempted to selectively breed plains zebras: they chose plains zebras which have fewer stripes and look slightly like quaggas. Baby zebras born to a slightly quagga-like mother and father may look more like the quagga, with a significantly reduced number of stripes. This project has achieved a certain level of success, producing several lovely baby zebras which have striking similarities to the quagga.

🔊 37

However, should we be happy about this? While this new generation of zebras is visually impressive, it only resembles the quagga in appearance. The fact is that these zebras are genetically different from quaggas. (3)The more we look at these young, cute, quagga-like zebras, the more we are forced to face the sad truth that the quagga died out because of our abuse of nature. Does this project help restore nature to its original state? Or is it just for the self-satisfaction of guilt-ridden human beings?

🔊 38

Furthermore, it is notable that people are interested in quaggas because they are beautiful in appearance. (4)It is said that good-looking endangered★ animals tend to attract attention and money from people, but that plain-looking endangered animals are often ignored. This suggests that human beings are biased towards beauty and ugliness even when it comes to environmental causes.

   ★ plains zebra「サバンナシマウマ」 endangered「絶滅の危険にさらされている」

❶ ....

❷ ....

....

❸ ....

❹ ....

....

❺ ....

....

❻ ....

| 語句 | 音声は、「英語」→「日本語の意味」の順で読まれます。 | CD 1・Tr 39 ～ 42 |

入試基本レベル

2	**zebra** [zí:brə]	
3	**stripe** [stráip]（名）	
6	**die out**	
7	**due to ～**	
10	**attractive** [ətræktiv]	
13	**close to ～**	
15	**slightly** [sláitli]	
17	**reduce** [ridʒú:s]	
21	**impressive** [imprésiv]	
21	**resemble** [rizémbl]	
21	**appearance** [əpíərəns]	
29	**suggest** [sʌgdʒést]	

入試標準レベル（共通テスト・私大）

2	**distinctive** [distíŋktiv]	
6	**trousers** [tráuzərz]	
10	**gather attention from ～**	
11	**conservation** [kÀnsərvéiʃən]	
12	**conduct** [kəndʌ́kt]（動）	
13	**it turns out that ...**	
13	**genetically** [dʒənétikəli]	
14	**attempt** [ətémpt]（動）	
14	**breed** [brí:d]（動）	
17	**significantly** [signífikəntli]	

18	**striking** [stráikiŋ]	
19	**similarity to ～**	
21	**visually** [víʒuəli]	
23	*be* **forced to** *do*	
23	**face** [féis]（動）	
24	**abuse** [əbjú:s]（名）	
25	**state** [stéit]（名）	状態
26	**furthermore** [fɔ́:rðərmɔ̀:r]	
29	**ignore** [ignɔ́:r]	
30	**when it comes to ～**	

入試発展レベル（二次・有名私大）

9	**revive** [riváiv]	生き返らせる
14	**selectively** [siléktivli]	選択的に
24	**restore ～ to ...**	～を…に戻す［復元する］
25	**self-satisfaction**	自己満足
26	**notable** [nóutəbl]	注目に値する

その他

2	**horse-like**	馬に似た
3	**brownish** [bráuniʃ]	茶色がかった
7	**overhunting** [òuvərhʌ́ntiŋ]	乱獲
7	**stuffed** [stʌ́ft]（形）	詰め物をした、剥製の
8	**specimen** [spésəmən]	標本、見本
25	**guilt-ridden**	罪の意識に苦しむ
27	**good-looking**	見た目のよい、美しい
28	**plain-looking**	見た目が地味な［美しくない］
29	*be* **biased towards ～**	～に対して偏見を抱いている
30	**ugliness** [ʌ́glinəs]	醜さ

本文解説 & Check Drill

1 【助動詞＋ have ＋過去分詞】(第 1 段落第 2 文)

Perhaps not, but you **may have seen** a zebra before.

▶ 〈may have＋過去分詞〉で「〜した(ことがある)かもしれない」。過去または完了した事柄に対する現在の推量を表す。上の例は、「あなたはシマウマを見たことがあるかもしれない」。

▶ 同様に過去について推量を表す表現には、〈must have＋過去分詞〉「〜したに違いない」、〈can't have＋過去分詞〉「〜したはずがない」、〈should have＋過去分詞〉「〜したはずだ」などがある。(〈should have＋過去分詞〉は「〜すべきだった(のに)」の意味でもよく用いられる。)

2 【those who ...】(第 2 段落第 3 文)

Those who would like to see the animals walk around the savannas again have conducted the Quagga Project for over thirty years in South Africa.

▶ 上の文では Those ... again までが主部となっている。この those は「人々」を意味し、those who ... で「…する人々」を意味する。主部の意味は「クアッガが再びサバンナを歩き回るのを見たいと思う人々」。

3 【The ＋比較級 ... , the ＋比較級 〜】(第 3 段落第 4 文)

The more we look at these young, cute, quagga-like zebras, **the more** we are forced to face the sad truth that the quagga died out because of our abuse of nature.

▶ 〈The ＋比較級 ..., the ＋比較級 〜〉の構文で、「…すればするほど、ますます〜する」を意味する。普通、... と〜には、〈S＋V ...〉の語順の文がくる。

Check Drill　1 は空所に適切な語を入れ、2 〜 4 は語句を並べ替え、5 は誤りを訂正して全文を書き直しなさい。

1. その問題が難しければ難しいほど、私はますます解けそうにない。 (畿央大)

   The more difficult the problem is, the (　　　　　) likely I am to solve it.

2. 努力家は成功する。 (中央大・改)

   Success (give their all / those / comes / who / to).

   ....

3. 彼の父親はその知らせにたいへん驚いたにちがいない。 (札幌大)

   His father (been / must / at / have / very surprised) the news.

   ....

4. 生活に困っている人々の手助けをしましょう。 (愛知医科大)

   Let's help (it / find / those / difficult / make / who / to) a living.

   ....

5. The more it is dangerous, the more I like it. (和光大・改)

   ....

展開	段落	要旨
導入	1	クアッガはシマウマ科の一種で、茶色がかった色をし、首と前半身の周りに（①　　　　　　　）を持つ。彼らはアフリカ南部で生息していたが、（②　　　　　　）のため19世紀に絶滅した。
本論①	2	研究者たちはクアッガを「（③　　　　　　　）」ようと、南アフリカで30年以上クアッガ・プロジェクトを行ってきた。彼らはしまがより少ない、クアッガに少し似た（④　　　　　　　　）を選択的に繁殖させた。その赤ちゃんは、しまの数がかなり減っており、クアッガに著しく似ているものもいる。
本論②	3	新しい世代のシマウマは、外見がクアッガに似ているだけで、（⑤　　　　　　　）にはクアッガと異なる。この計画は、クアッガを絶滅させたという罪の意識に苦しむ人間の自己満足にすぎないのではないか。
本論③	4	外見の美しさから、人々がクアッガに関心を寄せている点は注目すべきだ。対照的に、見た目が地味な絶滅危惧動物は、しばしば無視されると言われている。これは、環境保護においてさえも、人間が美醜に対して（⑥　　　　　　　）を持つことを示唆する。

■　以下を参考にして、「段落要旨」の下線部分を中心にまとめてみよう。

▶「導入」の内容（20〜30字）

【記述例】：「しま模様が特徴的なクアッガは…」

▶「本論①、②」の内容（40〜50字）

【言い換え例】：「クアッガ・プロジェクト」→「（クアッガの）再生計画」

▶「本論③」の内容（35〜45字）

（下書き）　　　　　　　　　　　　　　　　　　　10　　　　　　　　　　　　　　　　　　　20

（下書き用マス目）

10　　　　　　　　　　　　　　　　　　　20

（下書き用マス目）

CD 1
43

The host poured tea into the cup and placed it on the small table in front of his guests, who were a father and a daughter, and put the lid on the cup with a light sound. Apparently thinking of something, he hurried into the inner room, leaving the thermos* on the table. His two guests heard a chest of drawers opening and a rustling.

5 　　They remained sitting in the parlor*, the ten-year-old daughter looking at the flowers outside the window, the father just about to take his cup, when the crash came, right there in the parlor. Something was irreparably broken.

　　It was the thermos, which had fallen to the floor. The girl looked over her shoulder abruptly, startled, staring. (1)It was mysterious. Neither of them had touched it, not
10 even a little bit. True, it hadn't stood steadily when their host placed it on the table, but it hadn't fallen then.

　　(2)The crash of the thermos caused the host, with a box of sugar cubes in his hand, 44 to rush back from the inner room. He looked at the steaming floor and cried out, "It doesn't matter! It doesn't matter!"

15 　　The father started to say something. Then he muttered, "Sorry, I touched it and it fell."

　　"It doesn't matter," the host said.

　　Later, when they left the house, the daughter said, "Daddy, did you touch it?"

　　"No. But it stood so close to me."

20 　　"But you didn't touch it. I saw your reflection in the mirror. You were sitting perfectly still.

　　The father laughed. "What then would you give as the cause of its fall?"

　　"The thermos fell by itself. The floor is uneven. It wasn't steady when Mr. Li put it there. (3)Daddy, why did you say that you ..."

25 　　"(4)That won't do, girl. It sounds more acceptable when I say I knocked it down. 45 There are things which people accept less the more you defend them. (5)The truer the story you tell is, the less true it sounds."

　　The daughter was lost in silence for a while. Then she said, "Can you explain it only this way?"

30 　　"Only this way," her father said.

　　　* thermos「魔法びん」 parlor「客間」

❶ ....

❷ ....

❸ ....

❹ (4) .... (5) ....

❺ ....

語句 音声は、「英語」→「日本語の意味」の順で読まれます。　　CD 1 - Tr 46 ～ 49

入試基本レベル

1 **place** [pléis]（動）

3 **apparently** [əpǽrəntli]

3 **hurry** [hə́:ri]

6 **crash** [krǽʃ]（名）

9 **stare** [stéər]

14 **matter** [mǽtər]（動）

19 **close to ～**

22 **cause** [kɔ́:z]（名）

23 **by itself**

25 **acceptable** [əkséptəbl]

入試標準レベル（共通テスト・私大）

1 **pour** [pɔ́:r]

4 **drawer** [drɔ́:r]

6 **be about to do**

9 **mysterious** [mistíəriəs]

10 **steadily** [stédəli]

13 **rush** [rʌ́ʃ]（動）

20 **reflection** [riflékʃən]

25 **knock down**

26 **defend** [difénd]

28 **be lost**

28 **in silence**

入試発展レベル（二次・有名私大）

9 **startle** [stá:rtl]　　びっくりさせる

その他

2 **lid** [líd]　　ふた

4 **rustling** [rʌ́sliŋ]　　ガサガサという音

7 **irreparably** [irépərəbli]　　修復できないほど

9 **abruptly** [əbrʌ́ptli]　　急いで、慌てて

12 **sugar cube**　　角砂糖

15 **mutter** [mʌ́tər]（動）　　つぶやく

23 **uneven** [ʌní:vn]　　平らでない、水平でない

本文解説 & Check Drill

1 【hear ＋ O ＋現在分詞】(第1段落第3文)

His two guests **heard** a chest of drawers **opening** and a rustling.

▶ hear は知覚動詞として〈hear ＋ O ＋現在分詞〉の形をとり「O が〜するのを聞く」という意味になる。現在分詞の代わりに原形不定詞が用いられることもある。また O と続く動詞の関係が「受動」の場合は、過去分詞が用いられる。

2 【前置詞の as】(第7段落第2文)

"What then would you give **as** the cause of its fall?"

▶ as は主に接続詞として用いられるが、前置詞として「〜として」という意味で用いられることも多い。as の後には、上の例のように名詞が続くことが原則だが、動名詞や形容詞、前置詞句を導くこともある。

3 【the ＋比較級】(第8段落第4文)

The **truer** the story you tell is, **the less true** it sounds."

▶ 〈the ＋比較級 ...,the ＋比較級 〜〉の構文は「…であればあるほど、ますます〜」という意味になる。
▶ この構文は、語順にポイントがある。上の例は、The story you tell is true. という文と、It sounds true. という文が結ばれた形になっている。また、比較級の後が倒置されたり、be 動詞が省略されたりすることがある。

Check Drill 1〜4は語句を並べ替え、5は空所に適切なものを入れなさい。

1. 私たちは少女が古い歌を歌っているのを耳にした。 (長崎総合科学大)

We (girl / heard / old / a / singing / songs).

2. The more I tried to answer the question, the harder it seemed to become, until at (as / gave / I / it / last / up) impossible. (立教大)

3. 警官は男が何か言い訳をぶつぶつ言うのを聞いた。 (東洋大)

The police officer (man / as / heard / excuse / an / the / mutter / something).

4. 歳を重ねるほど新しい事を覚えるのが難しくなる。 (東京経済大)

The (get / the / it / you / older / harder / is / ,) for you to learn new things.

5. The lower we climbed down the mountains, ( ). (東海大)

① it got warmer　　　　　　② got it warmer
③ the warmer it got　　　　　④ warmer the got it

展開	段落	要旨
ある家を訪ねている父と娘	前半	父と娘はある家を訪れていた。家の主人は（①　　　　　）をカップに注いだあと、魔法びんをテーブルの上に置き、奥の部屋に行った。突然客間ですさまじい音がした。彼らは魔法びんに全く（②　　　　　）いなかったが、魔法びんは床に落ちて壊れた。音を聞いて主人が奥の部屋から戻ってきた。父は主人に、自分が（②　　　　　）落ちたのだと言って謝った。
父と娘の会話	後半	娘は父の発言を不審に思った。彼女は父が魔法びんに（②　　　　　）いなかったことを見ていた。娘は父にその理由を尋ねた。父は「本当のことを話せば話すほど、（③　　　　　　　　　　）のように聞こえる」ことがあるのだ、と説明した。

■　以下を参考にして、「段落要旨」の下線部分を中心にまとめてみよう。
　　▶「前半」の内容（45 ～ 55 字）
　　【言い換え例】：「彼らは魔法びんに全く～」→「魔法びんが勝手に落ちた」
　　▶「後半」の内容（50 ～ 60 字）
　　【記述例】：「不審に思う娘に、父は～だと言った」

（下書き）

It is often thought that when humans first learned how to control fire, one of its major effects was to keep people warm, but (1)that idea wrongly implies that our pre-cooking ancestors would have had difficulty staying warm without fire. Chimpanzees survive nights exposed to long, cold rain-storms. Gorillas sleep uncovered in high, cool mountains. Every species other than humans can maintain body heat without fire. (2)When our ancestors first controlled fire, they would not have needed it for warmth, (A) fire would have saved them some energy in maintaining body temperature.

But the opportunity to be warmed by fire created new options. Humans are 🔊51 exceptional runners, far better than chimpanzees and gorillas, and perhaps better even than wolves and horses, at running long distances. The problem for most animals is that they easily become overheated when they run. A chimpanzee sits exhausted after only five minutes' hard exercise, breathing heavily and visibly hot, with sweat pouring out of its body. Most animals cannot develop a solution to this problem because they need something to maintain body heat during rest or sleep, such as a thick coat of hair. (3)This, of course, cannot be removed after exercise.

The best way to lose heat is not to have a lot of body hair in the first place. A 🔊52 scientist, Peter Wheeler, has long argued that (4)this may be why humans are "naked apes": a reduction in hair might have allowed them to avoid becoming overheated on the hot savanna. But early humans could have lost their hair only if they had had an alternative system for maintaining body heat at night. Fire offers such a system. Once our ancestors controlled fire, they were able to keep warm even when they were resting. The benefit must have been high: the loss of their hair probably made humans better able to travel long distances during hot periods, when most animals are (B). They could then run for long distances when hunting animals. By allowing body hair to be lost, the control of fire increased humans' ability to run long distances making them better able to hunt or steal meat from rival species.

1 ....

....

2 ....

....

3 ....

....

4 ....

....

5 (A) .... (B) ....

6 ....

語句 音声は、「英語」→「日本語の意味」の順で読まれます。　　　　CD 1 - Tr 53 ～ 55

入試基本レベル	
1	**control** [kəntróul]（動）
2	**effect** [ifékt]（名）
2	**keep O C**
3	**ancestor** [ǽnsestər]
4	**survive** [sərváiv]
5	**species** [spíːʃiːz]
5	**maintain** [meintéin]（動）
9	**opportunity** [ɑ̀ːpərt(j)úːnəti]
13	**exercise** [éksərsàiz]（名）
16	**thick** [θík]
16	**remove** [rimúːv]
18	**argue** [ɑ́ːrgjuː]
19	**allow O to** *do*
19	**avoid** *doing*
21	**offer** [ɔ́(ː)fər]（動）
24	**period** [píəriəd]
27	**steal** [stíːl]

入試標準レベル（共通テスト・私大）	
2	**imply** [implái]
4	**expose A to B**
7	**warmth** [wɔ́ːrmθ]
7	**body temperature**
9	**option** [ɑ́ːpʃən]
10	**exceptional** [eksépʃənl]
12	**exhaust** [egzɔ́ːst]
14	**pour out**
14	**solution** [səlúːʃən]
19	**reduction** [ridʌ́kʃən]
21	**alternative** [ɔːltə́ːrnətiv]

入試発展レベル（二次・有名私大）	
12	**overheat** [òuvərhíːt]	～を過熱する
13	**visibly** [vízəbli]	明らかに
18	**naked** [néikid]	裸の
25	**inactive** [inǽktiv]	活動していない

本文解説 & Check Drill

---

1 【that 節を用いた形式主語構文】（第 1 段落第 1 文）

It is often thought that when humans first learned how to control fire, one of its major effects was to keep people warm,...

▶ 接続詞 that が導く名詞節が主語の働きをする場合、しばしば形式主語 It を文頭に置き、that 以下は文の終わりにまわすことがある。

▶ It の次には多くの場合〈It is ＋名詞［形容詞］〉となることが多いが、上の例のように、受動態や be 動詞以外の動詞が来ることもある。

2 【with を伴う分詞構文】（第 2 段落第 4 文）

A chimpanzee sits exhausted after only five minutes' hard exercise, breathing heavily and visibly hot, with sweat pouring out of its body.

▶ 〈with ＋名詞＋分詞〉で「～（名詞）が…（分詞）の状態で」という意味になる。with sweat pouring の分詞 pouring の意味上の主語は sweat なので、文の主語（A chimpanzee）と意味上の主語が異なる独立分詞構文に with が伴われていると考えてもよい。

▶ 付帯状況を表す with には〈with ＋名詞＋形容詞［前置詞句］〉の形になることも多い。

3 【接続詞 once】（第 3 段落第 5 文）

Once our ancestors controlled fire, they were able to keep warm even when they were resting.

▶ once は副詞として「一度」や「かつて」の意味で用いられることが多いが、副詞節を導く接続詞としての用法もある。「一度［いったん］～すれば」の意味になる。

Check Drill 　1～3 は語句を並べ替え、4 は空所に適切なものを入れ、5 は日本語に訳しなさい。

1. 君がいまだにご両親に経済的に頼っているとは驚きだ。　　　　　　　　　　　（名古屋市立大・改）

(are / that / still dependent / surprising / it / you / on / is) your parents for money.

....

2. 不幸なことに、私の座ったテーブルの両隣は、タバコを吸う人だった。　　　（東京電機大・改）

Unfortunately, I was sitting at the table (side / smokers / either / with / on / of) me.

....

3. いったん何かをしようと心に決めたら、決心を変えてはいけない。　　　　　（東京情報大・改）

(decided / something / once / you / do / have / to), you should never change your mind.

....

4. He lay on the sofa with his (　　　　) and soon fell asleep.　　　　　　（センター試験）

① arms folded 　　② arms folding 　　③ fold arms 　　④ folding arms

5. Once you attend the opera, you will understand its fascination.　　　　（同志社女子大・改）

....

展開	段落	要旨
序論	1	人間が火の（①　　　　　）方法を学んだとき、初めて自らを暖かくしておけるようになった、という考えは誤りだ。他の動物同様、火がなくても人間は（②　　　　　　）を保つことができていた。
本論	2	火の（①　　　　　）を覚えた人間は、他の動物に比べ（③　　　　　　）を走ることに優れている。多くの動物は走る際に、容易に（②　　　　）が高くなりすぎる。彼らは（②　　　　　）を維持するのに必要な（④　　　　　　　）があるために、この問題を解決できない。
結論	3	（②　　　　　）を下げるには、（④　　　　　　）を多く持たないことが最も有効だ。火を（①　　　　　）することで（②　　　　）を維持しやすくなった人間は、（④　　　　　　）をなくすことができた。結果、（③　　　　　）を走ると熱くなることが解決され、（⑤　　　　）や他の動物から肉を盗むことが上手になった。

■　以下を参考にして、「段落要旨」の下線部分を中心にまとめてみよう。
　　▶「序論」と「本論」の内容（40〜50字）
　　【記述例】：「火がなくても〜できていた人間は、…を覚えたことで」
　　▶「結論」の内容（55〜65字）
　　【記述例】：「〜がなくなったために、…が解決されたのだ」

（下書き）　　　　　　　　　　　　　　　　　　　　10　　　　　　　　　　　　　　　　　　　20

CD 1

Hita Gupta was heartbroken upon learning that her regular visits to nursing homes ✎56 were put on hold because of the coronavirus.

"They told me that I couldn't visit because they were trying to limit interaction with seniors to prevent the spread of the virus," Hita told CNN.

The 15-year-old had been volunteering at one facility near her home in Paoli, Pennsylvania, for more than a year — organizing activities like trivia quizzes and bingo for the residents.

"The seniors aren't able to see their families, so that's causing loneliness, boredom and anxiety," she said.

And then she thought of her own grandparents.

"They're in India but I have calls with them on Skype★. Even though they have to stay home, we can speak to them. The nursing home residents may not have that option," Hita explained.

So, she came up with the idea to send goodie bags★ — each one filled with one ✎57 large-print puzzle book, an adult coloring book, and coloring pencils.

"The puzzle and coloring books will help nursing home residents stimulate their minds and keep them occupied," said Hita.

The packages also include an encouraging note written by her 9-year-old brother, Divit. "My brother helps me a lot. It's a lot of work."

Hita coordinates with the nursing homes ahead of time to confirm that the bags can be received safely.

"I call them and say I'm going to leave the boxes outside the front door. They usually leave them out for a few days to make sure there aren't any germs★ before passing them out to the residents."

She has now sent packages to 23 nursing homes in the Philadelphia area.

"Cheering them up makes me happy. Even if it's just for one day."

Initially, Hita was purchasing items with her own pocket money, but figured if she ✎58 wanted to make a larger impact, she would need more money.

As news spread of her good deed, more people wanted to help.

"I've heard from a lot of people and people are sharing on social media. They've reached out saying, 'You've inspired me to do a similar project in my area.'"

The second-year high school student has created a GoFundMe★ account to help make even more of the thoughtful packages.

"(1)It makes me feel happy that she is able to give back to the community. She's able to let them know that they're not alone and there's a community that stands with them. I am very proud," Hita's mom, Swati, said.

The teenager says she will continue doing this until the public health crisis is over.

"Loneliness is now a bigger problem than ever with our social distancing guidelines.

(2)We need to let nursing home residents know that they are not being forgotten, and that they are not alone. As a community, we need to work together to make seniors feel loved and valued."

　＊　Skype「インターネット通話サービス」　goodie bag「（品物などの）詰め合わせ」
　　germ「病原菌」　GoFundMe「募金をするために用いるインターネット・サービス」

1
2
3

4
5

| 語句 | 音声は、「英語」→「日本語の意味」の順で読まれます。 | | CD 1 - Tr 59 ～ 62 |

入試基本レベル

3	**limit** [límit]（動）	
6	**organize** [ɔ́:rgənàiz]	
8	**cause** [kɔ́:z]（動）	
14	**come up with** ～	
14	*be* **filled with** ～	
20	**ahead of** ～	
23	**make sure (that)** ～	
24	**pass** ～ **out**	
26	**cheer** [tʃíər]	
27	**figure** [fígjər]（動）	
28	**impact** [ímpækt]	
31	**reach out**	

入試標準レベル（共通テスト・私大）

1	**regular** [régjələr]	
1	**nursing home**	
2	**put** ～ **on hold**	
4	**senior** [sí:njər]（名）	
4	**virus** [váiərəs]	
5	**facility** [fəsíləti]	
7	**resident** [rézidənt]	
8	**loneliness** [lóunlinəs]	
8	**boredom** [bɔ́:rdəm]	
9	**anxiety** [æŋzáiəti]	
11	**even though** ～	
13	**option** [ápʃən]	

16	**stimulate** [stímjəlèit]	
18	**encouraging** [inkʌ́:ridʒiŋ]（形）	
20	**confirm** [kənfə́:rm]	
26	**even if** ～	
27	**initially** [iníʃəli]	
31	**inspire O to** *do*	
33	**thoughtful** [θɔ́:tfəl]	
34	**community** [kəmjú:nəti]	
37	**crisis** [kráisis]	
41	**valued** [vǽlju:d]	

入試発展レベル（二次・有名私大）

3	**interaction with** ～	～との交流
17	**occupied** [ákjəpàid]（形）	夢中になって、忙しくして
20	**coordinate with** ～	～と連携する、協調する
29	**deed** [dí:d]	行い、行動

その他

1	**heartbroken** [há:rtbròukən]	悲しみに打ちひしがれた
2	**coronavirus** [kəróunəvàiərəs]	コロナウイルス
6	**trivia** [tríviə]	雑学知識、豆知識
15	**large-print**	大きな活字の
15	**coloring book**	塗り絵の本
37	**public health**	公衆衛生
38	**social distancing**	社会的距離を置くこと、感染拡大を防ぐために物理的な距離をとること

本文解説 & Check Drill

1 【独立分詞構文】 (第 7 段落)

So, she came up with the idea to send goodie bags — **each one filled with one large-print puzzle book, an adult coloring book, and coloring pencils.**

▶ 上記の文では、ダッシュ (—) 以下は直前の goodie bags の中身について具体的に説明している。主節の主語と異なる主語で始まる分詞構文である「独立分詞構文」と考えられる。

▶ each one は each goodie bag の意味で、過去分詞 filled (being filled の being が省略されたもの) の意味上の主語である。文にすれば each one was filled with ... となる。

2 【help + O + (to) *do*】 (第 8 段落)

The puzzle and coloring books will **help nursing home residents stimulate** their minds and **keep them occupied**...

▶ 〈help + O + (to) *do*〉 の形で「O が〜するのを手伝う、O が〜するのに役立つ」の意味を表す。keep them の前には will help が省略されている (will だけが省略されているとも考えられる)。keep them occupied で「自分たち (=老人ホームの入居者) を夢中にさせる」。

▶ help の目的語は「人」が原則であることに注意しよう。「私は妹の宿題を手伝った」は、˟ I helped my sister's homework. は誤りで、I helped my sister (to) do her homework. あるいは I helped my sister with her homework. と表現する。

3 【even though 〜 と even if 〜】 (第 6 段落第 2 文、第 13 段落第 1、2 文)

A. **Even though** they have to stay home, we can speak to them.

B. "Cheering them up makes me happy. **Even if** it's just for one day."

▶ even though 〜 は「〜だけれども」という意味で、実際に起こったことや、事実に対しての「譲歩」を表す。though の強調と考えてよい。

▶ even if 〜 は「たとえ〜だとしても」という「仮定」の意味を表す。if の強調と考えてよい。実際に起こっていないことについても述べることができる。

Check Drill　　1〜3 は空所に入る適切なものを選び、4、5 は語句を並べ替えなさい。

1. The novelist made a very long speech, the audience (　　) to feel bored. (駒澤大)
　① begun　　　　② had been begun　　③ beginning　　　④ to be beginning

2. I wonder if you can help me (　　) a watch I'd like to buy. (麗澤大)
　① finding　　　② to have find　　　③ to be found　　④ find

3. It is important not to give out your credit card number to anyone over the phone (　　) you know who you are talking to. (日本大)
　① so that　　　② even if　　　　③ but　　　　　④ or

4. 温かいミルクを飲めばよく眠れるかもしれない。 (関西学院大)
Drinking (milk / you / may / soundly / hot / sleep / help).

5. 厚手のコートを着ていたのに、寒かったです。 (立正大・改)
I (wearing / cold / was / though / felt / a heavy coat / even / I).

展開	段落	要旨
前編	1〜6	アメリカの高校生ヒタ・グプタは、コロナウイルスの感染のため、老人ホームへの訪問が今までのようにできなくなることを知った。家族に会えない（①　　　　　　　　　）の孤独や退屈、不安を思って彼女は心を痛めた。自分はインドにいる祖父母とはスカイプで話せるが、（①　　　　　　　　　）はそれもできないかもしれない、と彼女は思った。
中編	7〜13	ヒタは、（①　　　　　　　　　）の心を刺激し、夢中にさせるようなパズル本や塗り絵本などを入れた詰め合わせ袋を送ることにした。老人ホームとは（②　　　　　　　　　）連絡を取り、感染防止の対策もした。これまでに、彼女は 23 の老人ホームに詰め合わせ袋を送った。（①　　　　　　　　　）を励ますことは、彼女にとってもうれしいことだった。
後編	14〜20	（③　　　　　　　　　　　　　）によってヒタの活動が広く知られるようになり、多くの人から支持や激励の声が届いた。高齢者の（④　　　　　　　）は今まで以上に大きな問題だ。地域社会とともに、「高齢者自身が愛されている」と感じられる活動を行うことが必要だ、とヒタは考えている。

■　以下を参考にして、「段落要旨」の下線部分を中心にまとめてみよう。

▶　「前編」の内容（20〜30字）【記述例】：「高校生ヒタは〜を知り、〜と思った」

▶　「中編」の内容（20〜30字）【記述例】：「ヒタ〜をすることにした」

▶　「後編」の内容（30〜40字）【記述例】：「ヒタの活動は〜」

（下書き）　　　　　　　　　　　　　　　　　　　　　10　　　　　　　　　　　　　　　　　　　20

（空欄の原稿用紙マス）

10　　　　　　　　　　　　　　　　　　　20

（空欄の原稿用紙マス）

CD 1
🔊63

The current minimum wage in the United States is $7.25 per hour. That means that a person working full time (40 hours per week) earns $290 per week, or $15,080 per year. In most parts of the country, this is not enough to pay for basic necessities. In Philadelphia, for example, the average rent for a one-bedroom apartment is more than $1,600 per month. A person working full time at minimum wage in Philadelphia simply cannot afford to live there. I believe that the minimum wage should be replaced by a 'living wage' which would provide a full-time worker with enough income to live on.

We haven't always had (1)this problem. In the early 1970s, even the lowest-paid employees earned enough money to provide for themselves, and (2)far fewer families required two incomes in order to live comfortably. Even though workers are more productive today, wages have remained about the same. In the meantime, the cost of necessities (such as housing, health care, child care, education, and transportation) has increased greatly. In short, wages have not kept up with the cost of living.

Those in favor of a living wage, which would vary depending on the cost of living in a particular city, believe that earning a living wage should be guaranteed as a human right. Everyone has the right to be paid fairly for their labor, they say. They also claim two economic benefits of a living wage. First, a living wage would reduce the number of people receiving money from the government to buy necessities. This reduces the financial burden on taxpayers. Second, if people have more money, they are likely to spend it in their local communities, buying the items they need from local businesses. (3)This, supporters suggest, will increase profits, create jobs, and strengthen local economies.

Those against a living wage argue that the economic effects on local businesses and economies could be very negative. (4)They point to the burden placed on small businesses. If a fast food restaurant, for example, is required to raise the hourly wage of all of its employees by as much as 40%, the owners will be forced to raise prices to cover their increased costs. Some companies may be forced to cut jobs, while others may have to close completely because they can no longer remain competitive and make a profit. Under these conditions, local economies are likely to suffer as prices increase and employment decreases.

Some cities have already passed living wage laws, which require local employers to pay employees at a rate that is much higher than the minimum wage. However, these laws have only recently been put into action, and it is too soon to judge their effectiveness. More data are needed in order to determine if these laws improve the lives of working people.

🔊64

🔊65

🔊66

🔊67

❶ ....

❷ ....

....

❸ ....

....

❹ ....

❺ ....

....

❻ ....

入試基本レベル

7	replace [ripléis]	
7	provide ～ with ...	
8	income [ínkʌm]	
10	employee [implɔ́ii:]	
10	provide for ～	
11	comfortably [kʌ́mfərtəbli]	
13	transportation [trænspərtéiʃən]	
14	keep up with ～	
15	vary [véəri]	
15	depending on ～	
16	particular [pərtíkjələr]	
17	human right	
18	claim [kléim]（動）	
18	benefit [bénəfit]（名）	
18	reduce [ridú:s]	
22	supporter [səpɔ́:rtər]	
24	argue [á:rgju:]	
24	effect [ifékt]（名）	
25	negative [négətiv]（形）	
26	raise [réiz]（動）	
30	suffer [sʌ́fər]	
31	employment [implɔ́imənt]	
34	judge [dʒʌ́dʒ]（動）	

35	effectiveness [iféktivnəs]	
35	improve [imprú:v]	

入試標準レベル（共通テスト・私大）

1	current [kə́:rənt]（形）	
1	minimum [míniməm]	
1	wage [wéidʒ]	
12	productive [prədʌ́ktiv]	
12	in the meantime	
14	in short	
15	in favor of ～	
16	guarantee [gærəntí:]（動）	
20	financial [fainǽnʃəl]	
20	burden [bə́:rdn]（名）	
22	profit [práfət]（名）	
23	strengthen [stréŋkθn]	
29	competitive [kəmpétətiv]	
32	pass [pǽs]（動）	
34	put ～ into action	
35	determine [ditə̀:rmin]	

入試発展レベル（二次・有名私大）

1	per ～	～当たり
3	basic necessities	生活必需品

1 【部分否定】(第2段落第1文)

We **haven't always** had this problem.

▶ 通常、否定文で用いられる not は文全体を否定するが、いくつかの副詞や形容詞を含む文においては、not が文全体ではなく、その副詞や形容詞だけを否定する場合がある。これを、「部分否定」という。

▶ 「部分否定」になる文に含まれる語は「全部」や「常に」などの意味を表すもので、副詞では always、necessarily などが、形容詞では every、all、both などが挙げられる。

2 【目的を表す不定詞の副詞的用法】(第2段落第2文)

…, and far fewer families required two incomes **in order to** live comfortably.

▶ to 不定詞の前に in order や so as が置かれる場合、その不定詞はもっぱら「目的」(〜するために) の意味で用いられる。

▶ 「〜しないために」という否定形の「目的」を表す際は、in order *not* to、so as *not* to の語順になる。

▶ 意味上の主語を表す場合には、so as to は用いられず、in order *for* 〜 to となる。

3 【代名詞 those】(第3段落第1文)

Those in favor of a living wage, …, believe that earning a living wage should be guaranteed as a human right.

▶ 代名詞 those の後に、前置詞句や関係詞節が続く場合、その those は文中の複数名詞を指す。単数名詞の場合には that を用いる。

▶ 文中に those が指す名詞として文脈上適切なものがなく、突如として現れる those は、「人々」(people) の意味で使われる。

Check Drill　　1〜3は空所に適切なものを選んで入れ、4、5は語句を並べ替えなさい。

1. Some students were absent from the ceremony. (大阪教育大・改)

 = (　　　) students were present at the ceremony.

 ① None of the　　② Not all the　　③ No　　④ Not every

2. (　　　) become a doctor, you have to graduate from medical school. (杏林大)

 ① Enough to　　② With regard to　　③ By way of　　④ In order to

3. The customs of this country are quite different from (　　　) of Japan. (天理大)

 ① one　　② ones　　③ that　　④ those

4. 彼は電気を無駄に使わないように明かりを消した。 (東京医科大)

 He turned out the light (as / electricity / not / so / to / waste).

---

5. 他人に親切である人々はみんなに愛される。 (九州国際大)

 (who / others / kind / to / are / those) are loved by everybody.

展開	段落	要旨
序論	1	米国の現在の（①　　　　　　　）は、生活必需品をまかなうのに十分ではない。それらは、常勤の人々が暮らしていけるだけの収入を提供する「（②　　　　　　　）」に置き換えられるべきだ。
本論①	2	以前は、（①　　　　　　　）だけで生活できた。しかし現在、賃金は当時とほぼ同じであるにもかかわらず、必要な（③　　　　　　　）が大幅に増加しているのだ。
本論②	3	（②　　　　　　　）に賛成する人々は、2つの（④　　　　　　　）利点があると主張する。納税者への（⑤　　　　　　　）負担の軽減と、地域経済活性化の可能性だ。
本論③	4	（②　　　　　　　）に反対する人々は、それが地域経済にとって悪影響だと主張する。（②　　　　　　　）の導入は、人件費の高騰を意味し、価格上昇や（⑥　　　　　　　）悪化を招くおそれがある、と彼らは考えている。
結び	5	すでに（②　　　　　　　）法を制定した都市もあるが、その（⑦　　　　　　　）を判断するにはまだ早い。

■　以下を参考にして、「段落要旨」の下線部分を中心にまとめてみよう。
　▶「序論」の内容（65〜75字）
　▶「本論②、③」の内容（25〜35字）
　【言い換え例】：「〜に賛成する人々は…と主張する。〜に反対の人々は…と言う」→「〜には賛否両論がある」

（下書き）　　　　　　　　　　　　　　　　　10　　　　　　　　　　　　　　　　　20

10　　　　　　　　　　　　　　　　　20

Born and raised on the very poor island of Makoko in Nigeria, Noah Shemede can still remember when he first held a bottle of Coca-Cola in his hand. He tasted the drink ten years ago, on his ninth birthday, after his parents had made a special trip just to buy a bottle of it for him. However, he did not enjoy that first mouthful. "I thought it was awful," Noah said laughing.

(1)Across Africa, global brands like Coca-Cola were once rarely seen in places such as Makoko, where people were too poor to buy expensive brand-name goods. Now though, things are changing. Sub-Saharan Africa has experienced ten years of strong economic growth, and people's standard of living has risen as a result. The brand-name goods that you can see in the supermarkets of rich countries are becoming more common. Big global companies expect Africa to keep on developing in the future.

Today, Noah Shemede's sister Fatima sells Coca-Cola, Fanta and Sprite, along with home-fried snacks, from her canoe. The price is still high for local people. "These are not drinks for everyday drinking. Adults buy them for special occasions," she said. Another sign of change in Makoko that she tells us about is that families sometimes eat Nisshin instant noodles rather than traditional food like cow-tongue soup with rice.

All over the African continent, global companies interested in Africa's growth are trying to increase their sales. In Cameroon, Irish Guinness beer, famous for its rich flavor, has become an unexpected hit even in the countryside. Villagers like to mix it with local wine, to give it more taste and color. In Kenya and Nigeria, Samsung's solar-powered mobile phones are very popular. In Ivory Coast's cities, and even in the poor districts, (2)it is common to see youths selling Nestlé coffee in small cups, so that locals can afford to buy some.

Swiss-based Nestlé, which is one of the biggest global coffee and sweets companies, has been very successful in Africa recently. One reason for this is that it has used local sales agents. The people who own the family-run shops, which are so common in Africa, prefer to deal with people they know. In this way, Nestlé has doubled the number of African shops selling its products during the last year. Now, nearly half of its yearly profits come from developing countries, and Africa is an especially important market.

This trend is not all positive. (3)Not everyone thinks it is a good thing for the world's richest companies to make their profits in the world's poorest countries. After all, these companies can damage local producers of similar products, and probably poor people would be better off spending their limited money on health, education, and technology rather than on costly brand-name products. But all the same, the increasing consumption of global brands does show that Africa is getting richer, and this can only be good for its many poor people.

1

2

3

4 (1) .... (2) .... (3) .... (4) ....

語句 音声は、「英語」→「日本語の意味」の順で読まれます。　　　　　CD 2 - Tr 7 ～ 10

入試基本レベル

1 **raise** [réiz]（動）

6 **rarely** [réərli]

8 **experience** [ikspíəriəns]（動）

9 **economic growth**

9 **as a result**

11 **common** [kámən]（形）

11 **keep on** *doing*

13 **along with** ～

14 **local** [lóukəl]（形）

17 **rather than** ～

17 **traditional** [trədíʃənl]

20 **increase** [inkrí:s]（動）

21 **flavor** [fléivər]（名）

21 **mix ... with** ～

25 **can afford to** *do*

27 **successful** [səksésfl]

28 **own** [óun]（動）

29 **prefer** [prifə́:r]

31 **developing country**

32 **especially** [espéʃəli]

33 **positive** [pázətiv]（形）

35 **after all**

入試標準レベル（共通テスト・私大）

5 **awful** [ɔ́:fl]

15 **occasion** [əkéiʒən]

21 **unexpected** [ʌ̀nikspéktid]（形）

24 **district** [dístrikt]（名）

28 **agent** [éidʒənt]

29 **deal with** ～

31 **profit** [prá:fət]（名）

36 **limited** [límitid]

37 **all the same**

38 **consumption** [kənsʌ́mpʃən]

入試発展レベル（二次・有名私大）

4 **mouthful** [máuθfùl]　　ひとくち（分の量）

9 **standard of living**　　生活水準

その他

14 **canoe** [kənú:]　　カヌー

28 **family-run shop**　　家族経営の店

1 【too ... to 不定詞】（第 2 段落第 1 文）

Across Africa, global brands like Coca-Cola were once rarely seen in places such as Makoko, where people were **too** poor **to** buy expensive brand-name goods.

▶ 〈too ... to 不定詞〉は程度を表す、不定詞の副詞的用法である。「あまりにも…なので〜できない」の意味になる。節に書き換える場合は〈so ... that S cannot V〉になる。上の例では、people were so poor that they could not buy ... となる。

▶ 不定詞に意味上の主語が伴う場合は、〈for ＋名詞〉の形で表す。

2 【接続詞 so that】（第 4 段落第 5 文）

…, it is common to see youths selling Nestlé coffee in small cups, **so that** locals can afford to buy some.

▶ 〈so that〉は目的を表す副詞節を導く接続詞である。「〜するように、〜するために」と訳す。節の中には、上の例のように can や may、will などの助動詞が用いられることが多い。

▶ so that 節は in order to *do* や so as to *do* を使って書き換えることができる。上の例では in order for locals to be able to afford to buy some. となる。ただし so as to *do* は in order to *do* と異なり、意味上の主語（ここでは for locals）を置けないことに注意。

▶ so that 節は結果を表す副詞節としても用いられる。

3 【強調の do】（第 6 段落第 4 文）

But all the same, the increasing consumption of global brands **does show** that Africa is getting richer …

▶ 動詞は really や actually などの副詞でも強調できるが、助動詞の do を伴って〈do[does][did] ＋動詞の原形〉という形でも強調できる。「確かに〜する」などと訳す。

Check Drill　　1、2 は語句を並べ替え、3、4 は空所に適切なものを入れ、5 は不定詞を用いて書き換えなさい。

1.　天井は私でも手が届かないほど高かった。　　　　　　　　　　　　　　　　　　　　　　　　（東京経済大）

The ceiling was (for / high / me / to / too / touch).

2.　始発列車に間に合うように私は早起きをした。　　　　　　　　　　　　　　　　　　　　　　（広島修道大）

I got up early (be / I / in / might / so / that) time for the first train.

3.　We left early (　　　　) to avoid heavy traffic on the roads.　　　　　　　　　　　　　　（岩手医科大）

① as for　　　　　　② as in　　　　　　③ so as　　　　　　④ so that

4.　She doesn't talk much, but once she (　　　　) speak she is eloquent.　　　　　　　　　　（城西大）

① will　　　　　　② shall　　　　　　③ does　　　　　　④ did

5.　This question is so difficult that no one can answer it.　　　　　　　　　　　　　　　　　（中京大・改）

展開	段落	要旨
導入	1	あるアフリカの子どもは、初めて（①　　　　　　　　　　）を飲んだときのことを 10 年経った今でも覚えている。
本論①	2	サハラ砂漠以南のアフリカ諸国の（②　　　　　　　　　　）のおかげで、アフリカにおいて（③　　　　　　　　　）商品は一般的になってきた。
本論②	3	地元の人々にとって、（③　　　　　　　　　）商品はまだ高価すぎるので、日常的なものではない。
本論③	4	（④　　　　　　　　　　）企業はアフリカで売り上げを伸ばしたいと考えている。
本論④	5	（⑤　　　　　　　　）社はアフリカで成功をおさめている。知人との取引を好む現地の店のために、地元の販売業者を使ったことが成功理由の１つだ。
結論	6	この傾向に否定的な意見もあるが、それはアフリカの豊かさを示し、多くの（⑥　　　　　　　　　）人々にとってはよいことである。

百字要約　　「段落要旨」を参考にして、本文全体の内容を百字程度の日本語で要約しなさい。

■　以下を参考にして、「段落要旨」の下線部分を中心にまとめてみよう。
　▶「導入」の内容は「具体的なエピソード」のため、ここでは省略。
　▶「本論①」の内容（35 〜 45 字）
　▶「結論」の内容（55 〜 65 字）

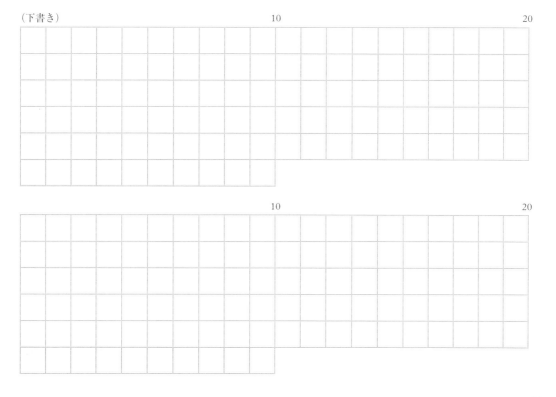

（下書き）

CD 2
11

A coral reef* is made up of many coral colonies all living together. The reef may
stretch hundreds of miles across, but it is constructed by coral polyps* only a quarter
of an inch or less in size. The reef itself is a living, growing organism — colonies of
tiny animals all working together to create the largest structures on Earth. This is
one of the most complex and mysterious ecosystems* known to mankind, and it all
works because of the tiny animals that produce the huge reef structure.

12

Over half a billion years ago, before there was any life on land, the seas contained
primitive coral reefs, consisting of sponges* and primitive corals. (1)This means that
coral reefs are among the oldest complex natural communities still in existence on
Earth. While many changes and extinctions in reefs have occurred throughout their
history, reefs have survived. In fact, some coral reef animals known today are
almost unchanged from those found in fossils dating from the age of dinosaurs, 100
million years ago. (2)Coral reefs are wonderful to see, and rich gardens in the sea,
supporting an astonishing amount of marine life in a densely packed, thriving marine
metropolis. In fact, coral reefs have the largest abundance and greatest diversity of
life living together of any place on Earth, including the tropical rain forests. (3)People
often refer to coral reefs as "rainforests of the sea."

13

In an area with this much diversity of life, it is easy to think that the tropical
oceans are highly rich in nutrients. (4)This is the popular misunderstanding.
Compared to the cold, murky waters of the temperate seas, tropical seas limit the
number of animal plankton, which makes their water clear, yet with very low food
resources. Thus, coral reefs live in nearly sterile* water. A coral reef is a gathering
place in the ocean. (5)It is an oasis in a desert, a place which gives shelter and food
in an ocean where these things are rare. In fact, the entire tropical ocean ecosystem
depends on the reef for sustenance.

* reef「礁（しょう）」 coral polyps「サンゴ虫」 ecosystem「生態系」
sponges「海綿動物」 sterile「不毛な」

1 ....

2 ....

3 ....

4 実際は、熱帯の海は ①[　　　　　　　　　　　　　　　　　　　　　　　　　　] のに、一般の人々
は ②[　　　　　　　　　　　　　　　　　　　　　　] と誤解している。

5 ....

6 ....

| 語句 | 音声は、「英語」→「日本語の意味」の順で読まれます。 | CD 2 - Tr 14 ～ 17 |

入試基本レベル

1	*be* made up of ～	
2	stretch [strétʃ]（動）	
4	create [kriéit]	
6	tiny [táini]	
6	huge [hjúːdʒ]	
7	contain [kəntéin]	
8	consist of ～	
10	occur [əkə́ːr]	
14	amount [əmáunt]（名）	
16	including ～	
17	refer to ～ as ...	
20	compared to ～	
20	limit [límit]（動）	
22	resource [ríːsɔ̀ːrs]（名）	
22	gather [ɡǽðər]（動）	
23	desert [dézərt]（名）	

入試標準レベル（共通テスト・私大）

1	colony [kɑ́ləni]	
2	construct [kənstrʌ́kt]（動）	
2	quarter [kwɔ́ːrtər]（名）	
3	organism [ɔ́ːrɡənìzm]	
4	structure [strʌ́ktʃər]（名）	
5	complex [kὰmpléks]	
5	mysterious [mistíəriəs]	
5	mankind [mænkáind]	

8	primitive [prímətiv]	
9	community [kəmjúːnəti]	
9	in existence	
10	extinction [ekstíŋkʃən]	
12	fossil [fɑ́sl]	
12	date from ～	
12	dinosaur [dáinəsɔ̀ːr]	
14	astonishing [əstɑ́niʃiŋ]	
15	abundance [əbʌ́ndəns]	
15	diversity [daivə́ːrsəti]	
16	tropical rain forest	
19	misunderstanding [mìsʌndərstǽndiŋ]	
23	shelter [ʃéltər]（名）	
24	entire [entáiər]	

入試発展レベル（二次・有名私大）

14	densely [dénsli]	密集して
14	thrive [θráiv]	繁栄する
15	metropolis [mətrɑ́pəlis]	大都市
19	nutrient [núːtriənt]（名）	栄養素
20	temperate [témpərət]	温帯の

その他

20	murky [mə́ːrki]	濁った
21	animal plankton	動物プランクトン
25	sustenance [sʌ́stənəns]	食物、食料

本文解説 & Check Drill

1 【譲歩を表す接続詞 while】（第 2 段落第 3 文）

While many changes and extinctions in reefs have occurred throughout their history, reefs have survived.

▶ 接続詞 while は「時」を表す場合は「～する間」という意味だが、対比的な 2 つの文をつないで「～に対して」、あるいは本例のように「～だけれども」という「譲歩」の意味になることもある。

2 【主節の後に続く分詞構文】（第 2 段落第 5 文）

Coral reefs are wonderful to see, and rich gardens in the sea, **supporting** an astonishing amount of marine life in a densely packed ...

▶ 文頭に分詞構文が置かれる場合は「～するとき」や「～なので」を表すことが多いが、主節の後にくる分詞構文は、主節の後に起こった動作を表したり、主節を補足する内容が続くのが一般的である。

3 【同格】（第 3 段落第 6 文）

It is **an oasis** in a desert, **a place** which gives shelter and food in an ocean where these things are rare.

▶ 同格は「一般的・抽象的・比喩的な名詞」の後に具体的な内容が続く形が多い。ここでは「名詞＋名詞」の形になっていて、an oasis in a desert を a place which ... が具体的に説明している。

Check Drill 　1～3 は語句を並べ替え、4、5 は空所に適切なものを入れて日本語に訳しなさい。

1. 自分には能力がないと思って、失望してはいけない。 （中京大・改）

   You must not be discouraged, (you / that / thinking / no / have) ability.

   ....

2. 私は 1 日中ベッドに寝ていて、自分の生活を改善する方法を夢見ていた。 （西南学院大・改）

   I stayed in bed all day long, (ways / improve / dreaming / my / about / to) life.

   ....

3. 科学者はなぜ地震が起こるかは知っているが、まだ地震を予知することはできない。 （亜細亜大・改）

   (know / earthquakes / scientists / happen / while / why), they are still not able to predict them.

   ....

4. The African elephant is the world's largest land animal, (　　　) up to 7,000 kilograms.

   ① weigh　　　② weighing　　　③ weighs　　　④ weighted 　（会津大）

   ....

5. Social science, (　　　) in 1998, is no longer taught at this college. 　（センター試験）

   ① studying the subject　　　　② having studied

   ③ the subject I studied　　　　④ I have studied

   ....

展開	段落	要旨
導入	1	サンゴ礁は、多数のサンゴの（①　　　　　　　）が共生しできている。
説明①	2	サンゴ礁は地球上に現存する最古の複雑な自然（②　　　　　　）の１つである。サンゴ礁は海中の肥沃な場所であり、多数の海洋生物を養っている。共生する生命の数とその種類の多さから「海の（③　　　　　　　）」とも呼ばれている。
説明②	3	サンゴ礁は、熱帯の海の生態系全体に（④　　　　　　）や住む場所を提供する、海のオアシスと言える。

百字要約　　「段落要旨」を参考にして、本文全体の内容を百字程度の日本語で要約しなさい。

■　以下を参考にして、「段落要旨」の下線部分を中心にまとめてみよう。
▶　「導入」の内容（15〜25字）
▶　「説明①」の内容（45〜55字）
▶　「説明②」の内容（30〜40字）

（下書き）

For some lizards it is easy being green. It is in their blood. Six species of lizards in New Guinea bleed lime green thanks to evolution gone weird. It is unusual, but there are creatures that bleed different colors of the rainbow besides red. The New Guinea lizards' blood — along with their tongues, muscles, and bones — appears green because of incredibly large doses of a green bile* pigment*. (1)The bile levels are higher than those at which other animals, including people, could survive.

Scientists still do not know why this happened, but evolution is providing some hints into this nearly 50-year mystery. By mapping the evolutionary family tree of New Guinea lizards, researchers found that green blood developed inside the amphibians — animals that can live both on land and in water — at four independent points in history, likely from a red-blooded ancestor, according to a study in Wednesday's journal *Science Advances*. (2)This is not a random accident of nature but suggests this trait of green blood gives the lizards an evolutionary advantage of some kind, said Christopher Austin of Louisiana State University. "Evolution can do amazing things given enough time," Austin said. "The natural world is a fascinating place."

Austin first thought that maybe being green and full of bile would make New Guinea lizards taste bad to potential predators. "I actually ate several lizards myself and they did not taste bad," Austin said. He also fed plenty of them to a paradise kingfisher bird with no ill effects except maybe a fatter bird.

Understanding bile is probably key. Blood cells do not last forever. After they break down, the iron is recycled for new red blood cells, but toxins are also produced, which is essentially bile. In the New Guinea lizards, levels of a green bile pigment are 40 times higher than what would be toxic in humans. It is green enough to overwhelm the color of the red blood cells and (A) everything green, Austin said. In people, elevated green bile pigment levels sometimes kill malaria parasites. Austin thinks that might be why lizards evolved to be green-blooded because malaria is an issue for New Guinea and lizards. It might be the result of evolution trying to kill the malaria parasite in lizards or it might be past lizards were infected so heavily that this was the body's reaction, he said.

Michael Oellermann, a researcher at the University of Tasmania in Australia, praised Austin's work and wondered if there is an evolutionary cost to having green blood. (3)Otherwise more creatures would bleed green or another color, he said.

> ★ bile「胆汁」 pigment「色素」

1 ....

2 ....
....

3 ....

4 ....
....

5 ....

語句　音声は、「英語」→「日本語の意味」の順で読まれます。　　　CD 2 - Tr 23 〜 26

入試基本レベル

#	語	意味
1	species [spí:ʃi(:)z]	
4	along with 〜	
11	ancestor [ǽnsestər]	
12	accident [ǽks(ə)dənt]	
13	advantage [ədvǽntidʒ]（名）	
15	amazing [əméiziŋ]	
21	forever [fərévər]（副）	
27	issue [íʃu:]（名）	
32	praise [préiz]（動）	
32	cost [kɔ́(:)st]（名）	

入試標準レベル（共通テスト・私大）

#	語	意味
1	lizard [lízərd]	
2	bleed [blí:d]（動）	
2	evolution [èvəlú:ʃən]	
3	creature [krí:tʃər]	
5	incredibly [inkrédəbli]	
6	survive [sərváiv]	
10	independent [indipéndənt]（形）	
12	random [rǽndəm]	行き当たりばったりの、偶然の
13	trait [tréit]	
15	fascinating [fǽsənèitiŋ]	

入試基本レベル（続き）

#	語	意味
18	potential [pəténʃəl]（形）	
21	last [lǽst]（動）	
23	essentially [isénʃəli]	
29	infect [infékt]	
33	otherwise [ʌ́ðərwàiz]	もしそうでなければ

入試発展レベル（二次・有名私大）

#	語	意味
2	weird [wíərd]（形）	奇妙な
8	evolutionary [èvəlú:ʃənèri]	進化の
19	feed 〜 to ...	〜（餌など）を…に与える
20	ill effect	悪影響
24	toxic [táksik]	有毒な
24	overwhelm [òuvərhwélm]	圧倒する
26	elevate [éləvèit]	高める、上昇させる
26	parasite [pǽrəsàit]	寄生虫、寄生動物

その他

#	語	意味
5	large doses of 〜	大量の〜
8	family tree	家系図
10	amphibian [æmfíbiən]	両生類
18	predator [prédətər]	捕食動物
22	break down	故障する、分解する
22	toxin [táksn]	毒素

本文解説 & Check Drill

1 【前置詞＋関係代名詞】（第1段落第6文）

The bile levels are higher than those **at which** other animals, including people, could survive.

▶ at which 以下は、前置詞が関係代名詞 which の前についた関係代名詞節。which の先行詞は those で、which は前置詞 at の目的語の働きをしている。

▶ those は前出の〈the ＋複数名詞〉の代わりをする代名詞で、ここでは those = the bile levels「胆汁の濃度」。

▶ could survive の could は仮定法過去で、「（もしも胆汁がその濃度であれば）生存できるだろう」の意味。

2 【倍数表現】（第4段落第4文）

In the New Guinea lizards, levels of a green bile pigment are **40 times higher than** what would be toxic in humans.

▶ 「〜の X 倍」は、〈X times as ＋原級 ＋ as 〜〉あるいは〈X times ＋比較級 ＋ than 〜〉の形で表される。上の例では、40 times higher than 〜と比較級の形が使われている。比較対象の what would be toxic in humans は関係代名詞節で、「人間において有毒となるようなもの」。この what は、those(= the levels) of a green bile pigment which の意味。

▶ would be toxic「有毒となるだろう」は仮定法過去で、in humans に「もしも人間の場合だったら［人間の中にあったら］」という仮定の意味が込められている。

3 【enough ＋ to 不定詞】（第4段落第5文）

It is green **enough to** overwhelm the color of the red blood cells and ...

▶〈形容詞・副詞 ＋ enough to *do*〉で、「〜するくらい十分に…、とても…なので〜できる」という意味を表す。

▶ enough は修飾するもので語順が変わり、名詞の場合には普通〈enough ＋名詞〉、形容詞または副詞の場合には必ず〈形容詞・副詞 ＋ enough〉の語順になる。

Check Drill 1〜3 は空所に入る適切なものを選び、4、5 は語句を並べ替えなさい。

1. Can you imagine the speed (　　　) the earth goes around the sun? （青山学院大）
　① which　　② at which　　③ in which　　④ where

2. I do not think the number of people (　　　) this rule applies is very large. （駒澤大）
　① to whom　　② whom　　③ of which　　④ in which

3. That sumo wrestler looks (　　　) as Mary. （東京経済大・改）
　① three much heavier　　　② three times heavier
　③ three times heavy　　　④ three times as heavy

4. その彫刻の実際の大きさは、写真の10倍くらいだろう。 （明海大）
　The actual size of the sculpture will be (in / than / ten / bigger / times) the photograph.

5. 昨年の冬、氷は上を歩けるほど厚かった。 （自治医科大）
　The ice was (enough / on / thick / to / walk) last winter.

展開	段落	要旨
序論	1	奇妙な進化の結果、ニューギニアに生息する6種のトカゲは血が黄緑色である。 彼らの血液は、大量の緑色の（①　　　　　　　）を含んでいる。
本論①	2	研究者たちはニューギニアのトカゲの進化の（②　　　　　　　）を作成することで、トカゲの体内で緑色の血液が、おそらくは赤い血液の祖先から生じたことを発見した。 緑色の血液はトカゲに何らかの進化上の利点を与えている、とオースティン氏は語った。
本論②	3	オースティン氏は最初、緑色をしていて大量の胆汁があるために、ニューギニアのトカゲは（③　　　　　　　）にとってまずいのだろうと考えたが、そうではなかった。
本論③	4	ニューギニアのトカゲにおける緑色の（①　　　　　　　）の濃度は、人間にとって有毒な量の（④　　　　）倍だ。人間の場合、緑色の（①　　　　　　　）の濃度が上がると（⑤　　　　　　　）の寄生虫が死ぬことがあるため、彼らは緑色の血液を持つように進化したのかもしれない、とオースティン氏は考えている。
本論④	5	緑色の血液を持つことには進化上の（⑥　　　　　　　）が伴う、と考えている研究者もいる。

- ■　以下を参考にして、「段落要旨」の下線部分を中心にまとめてみよう。
  - ▶「序論」の内容（30〜40字）
  - ▶「本論①」の内容（20〜30字）
  - 【言い換え例】：「緑色の血液が赤い血液の祖先から生じた」→「進化して緑色の血液を獲得した」
  - ▶「本論②」の内容は、「誤っていた仮説の紹介」であるため、ここでは省略。
  - ▶「本論③」の内容（35〜45字）　【記述例】：「それは（＝「本論①」の内容）〜であるからだと考える学者もいる」
  - ▶字数に余裕があれば、「本論④」の内容を含めてもよい。

（下書き）

CD 2
🔊 27

Since ancient times, historians have noticed that the rise and fall of civilizations is closely connected to population changes. These shifts in population have had (1)a significant effect on the destiny of societies. Shrinking populations have often given way militarily, economically, and culturally to expanding populations. Growing populations, particularly when geographically bound, have been the cause of many historical events. Among the historical changes brought about by population growth are political revolutions and national expansion.

🔊 28

Britain's expansion into the New World and the Industrial Revolution were both in many ways the result of Great Britain's large population growth rates in the 17th century. (2)Britain's population growth resulted in a widely held belief in the 18th and 19th centuries that it faced an unemployment crisis. To resolve the crisis, the government encouraged people to move abroad to its colonies in America and Australia. It also encouraged businesses to invest in new ideas as a way of creating jobs. Some of the new ideas eventually led to the technological breakthroughs of the Industrial Revolution.

🔊 29

Population growth in 18th-century France played a role in the French Revolution. France's population grew from 24.6 million in 1740 to 28.1 million in 1790. This helped increase the demand for food at a time of short supply, thereby driving up food prices throughout France. Price rises spread further as a result of urbanization and the increased circulation of money. Consequently, (3)the purchasing power of the average French wage earner was reduced, which caused a business downturn. The downturn hurt the growing and increasingly powerful French craftsman and merchant classes. This situation led to social unrest made worse by an unfair tax system, which failed to provide enough revenue to support public spending. This in turn led to financial ruin in 1787 and finally revolution in 1789.

🔊 30

Japanese expansion from the 1870s to 1945 was caused in part by Japan's rise in population. In the mid-19th century, the Japanese population grew rapidly. This came after a period of 150 years in which Japanese deliberately reduced their birth rates to slow growth. Growth led to fears about declining living standards and the need for more land. Japanese rulers took advantage of (4)these fears and gathered support for an expansionist policy. This included settling the northern islands of the archipelago and taking control of Okinawa, Taiwan and Korea.

❶

❷

❸

❹

❺ (1) .... (2) .... (3) ....

語句　音声は、「英語」→「日本語の意味」の順で読まれます。　　　　CD 2 - Tr 31 ～ 34

入試基本レベル

1 **civilization** [sìvələzéiʃən]

1 *be* **connected to ~**

6 **bring about ~**

7 **revolution** [rèvəl(j)ú:ʃən]

16 **result in ~**

18 **supply** [səplái]（名）

19 **as a result of ~**

21 **reduce** [rid(j)ú:s]

入試標準レベル（共通テスト・私大）

2 **shift** [ʃift]（名）

5 **geographically** [dʒì:əgrǽfikəli]

7 **expansion** [ekspǽnʃən]

11 **unemployment** [ʌ̀nimplɔ́imənt]

11 **crisis** [kráisis]

11 **resolve** [rizálv]

12 **encourage** [enkə́:ridʒ]

12 **colony** [káləni]

13 **invest in ~**

20 **circulation** [sə̀:rkjəléiʃən]

20 **consequently** [kánsəkwèntli]

20 **purchase** [pə́:rtʃəs]（動）

21 **wage** [wéidʒ]

22 **merchant** [mə́:rtʃənt]

25 **ruin** [rú(:)in]（名）

30 **take advantage of ~**

入試発展レベル（二次・有名私大）

3 **destiny** [déstəni]　　　運命

3 **shrink** [ʃríŋk]（動）　　縮む

14 **breakthrough** [bréikθru:]（名）　躍進

19 **urbanization** [ə̀:rbnizéiʃən]　都市化

28 **deliberately** [dilíbərətli]　意図的に

30 **ruler** [rú:lər]　　　支配者、統治者

その他

5 **bound** [báund]（形）　　縛り付けられた

21 **downturn** [dáuntə́:rn]　（景気などの）低迷

23 **unrest** [ʌnrést]　　　不安

24 **revenue** [révən(j)ù:]　税収、歳入

31 **archipelago** [à:rkəpéləgòu]　列島

本文解説 & Check Drill

1 【変化を表す前置詞 in】（第 1 段落第 2 文）

These shifts **in** population have had a significant effect on the destiny of societies.

▶ 何かの「変化」を示す場合、日本語では「人口の増加」のように「…の〜」と表すことが多いが、英語では「〜の」に前置詞の in がよく用いられる。

2 【lead to】（第 2 段落第 4 文）

Some of the new ideas eventually **led to** the technological breakthroughs of the Industrial Revolution.

▶ 〈lead to 〜〉は「（道などが）〜に通じている」が本体の意味だが、「…の結果〜になる」という意味として、主語に「原因」、前置詞 to 以下に「結果」がくる「無生物主語の構文」の動詞としてよく用いられる。to の後に動名詞がくることも多い。

3 【非制限用法の関係代名詞 which】（第 3 段落第 5 文）

Consequently, the purchasing power of the average French wage earner was reduced, **which** caused a business downturn.

▶ 関係代名詞の which には、直前の特定の名詞を先行詞とする通常の用法以外に、前文の内容（あるいはその一部）を先行詞とする用法がある。これは which だけに見られるものであり、必ずカンマのついた非制限用法になる。上の例では、the purchasing power of the average French wage earner was reduced が which の先行詞になっている。

| Check Drill | 1、2 は語句を並べ替え、3 〜 5 は空所に適切なものを入れなさい。 |

1. 電子コミュニケーションの普及によって、紙の手紙を書く人が減った。 （東海大・改）

The popularity of (to / people / has / electronic communication / writing / fewer / led) paper letters.

2. 父は毎朝 5 キロ走るつもりだと言ったが、私はそれは大胆すぎることだと思った。 （神奈川大・改）

My father said that he would run five kilometers every morning, (too / thought / which / ambitious / I / was).

3. There was a dramatic drop (　　　) temperature on the top of the mountain. （昭和大）

① to　　　　② with　　　　③ in　　　　④ for

4. The accident was due to his carelessness. （日本工業大・改）

= His carelessness (　　　) the accident.

① led to　　② resulted from　　③ was caused by　　④ called for

5. There are few places downtown for parking, (　　　) is really a problem. （センター試験）

① what　　　② where　　　③ which　　　④ that

展開	段落	要旨
主題	1	文明の盛衰は（①　　　　　　　）の変化と密接な関係がある。（①　　　　　　　）の増加は、多くの歴史的な出来事の原因となった。
具体例①	2	イギリスの（①　　　　　　　）増加は、新世界への進出や（②　　　　　　　　　　）をもたらした。
具体例②	3	フランスの（①　　　　　　　）増加は、（③　　　　　　　　　　　）の原因の１つとなった。
具体例③	4	1870 年代から 1945 年までの（④　　　　　　）の拡大は、（①　　　　　　　）増加による（⑤　　　　　　　　　）の低下や、広い土地の必要性へのおそれが一因だった。

■　以下を参考にして、「段落要旨」の下線部分を中心にまとめてみよう。
　▶「主題」の内容（20 〜 30 字）
　▶「具体例①〜③」の内容（75 〜 85 字）
　【記述例】：「具体例①や、具体例②、具体例③も〜が原因の１つだった」
　【言い換え例】：「1870 年代から 1945 年まで」→「明治から太平洋戦争まで」

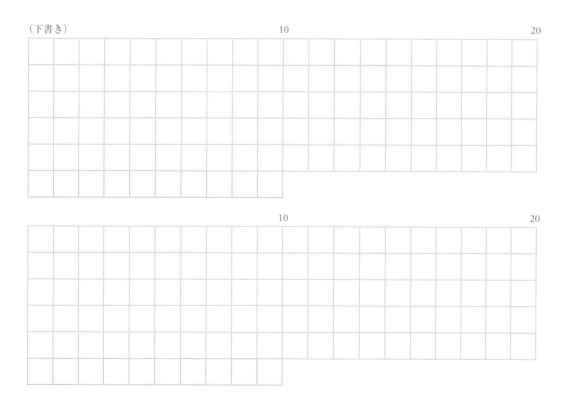

（下書き）

Most people know that the *Titanic* sank because it hit an iceberg★. However, ✎35
Donald Olson, an expert in physics, and a team of scientists have examined (1)the
role the moon may have played in the disaster. Since the *Titanic* sank in the early
hours of April 15, 1912, resulting in great loss of life, scholars have puzzled over why
5　Captain Edward Smith was not worried about warnings of icebergs nearby. Smith,
the most experienced captain in the White Star Line, had sailed the North Atlantic
sea lanes on numerous occasions. He had been assigned to the first voyage of the
Titanic because he was a knowledgeable and careful seaman.

Why had such a large number of icebergs floated into the shipping lanes so far ✎36
10　south that night? Olson and his team investigated one theory that an unusually close
approach by the moon in January, 1912 may have produced very high tides. As a
result, far more icebergs than usual managed to separate from Greenland, and floated,
still fully grown, south into the shipping lanes.

Olson said (2)a "once in many lifetimes" event occurred on January 4, 1912, when ✎37
15　the moon and sun lined up in such a way that their gravitational pulls★ increased
each other. At the same time, the moon's approach to Earth that January was the
closest it had been in 1,400 years. The point of closest approach occurred within six
minutes of the full moon. (3)On top of that, the Earth's closest approach to the sun
in a year had happened just the previous day. "This (4)arrangement of events increased
20　the moon's tide-raising power to the maximum," Olson said. Olson's research
determined that to reach the shipping lanes by mid-April, (5)(must / the *Titanic* / that /
the iceberg / into / have / crashed) broken off from Greenland in January, 1912. The
high tide caused by the strange combination of events would have been enough to
separate icebergs and keep them floating to reach the shipping lanes by April, he
25　said.

(6)The team's *Titanic* research may justify Captain Smith's choices by showing ✎38
that he had a good excuse for reacting so casually to a report of ice in the ship's path.
He had no reason at the time to believe that the icebergs he was facing were as
numerous or as large as they turned out to be, Olson said.

30　"The probability of all these variables lining up in just the way they did was, well,
hard to imagine," he concluded.

　★ iceberg「氷山」　gravitational pulls「引力」

1

....

....

2

....

3 (3) .... (4) ....

4 ....

5 ....

6 (1) .... (2) .... (3) ....

| 語句 | 音声は、「英語」→「日本語の意味」の順で読まれます。 | CD 2 - Tr 39 ～ 42 |

入試基本レベル

2	**expert** [ékspə:rt]（名）	
2	**examine** [igzǽmən]	
3	**play a role in ~**	
3	**disaster** [dizǽstər]	
4	**result in ~**	
6	**sail** [séil]（動）	
9	**a large number of ~**	
9	**float** [flóut]（動）	
10	**theory** [θíːəri]	
10	**unusually** [ʌnjúːʒuəli]	
11	**approach** [əpróutʃ]（名）	
14	**occur** [əkə́ːr]	
15	**increase** [inkríːs]（動）	
19	**arrangement** [əréindʒmənt]	
22	**crash** [krǽʃ]（動）	
24	**separate** [sépərèit]（動）	
24	**keep O doing**	
27	**excuse for ~**	
29	**turn out ~**	
31	**conclude** [kənklúːd]	

入試標準レベル（共通テスト・私大）

1	**sink** [síŋk]	
2	**physics** [fíziks]	
4	**puzzle over ~**	
5	**warning** [wɔ́ːrniŋ]（名）	

6	**experienced** [ekspíəriənst]	
7	**numerous** [n(j)úːmərəs]	
7	**occasion** [əkéiʒən]	
7	**assign** [əsáin]	
7	**voyage** [vɔ́i(i)dʒ]（名）	
10	**investigate** [invéstəgèit]	
11	**tide** [táid]（名）	
12	**than usual**	
12	**manage to do**	
15	**line up**	
18	**on top of ~**	
19	**previous** [príːviəs]	
20	**maximum** [mǽksəməm]	
21	**determine** [ditə́ːrmən]	
22	**break off**	
23	**combination** [kàmbənéiʃən]	
26	**justify** [dʒʌ́stəfài]	
30	**probability** [prɑ́:bəbiləti]	

入試発展レベル（二次・有名私大）

8	**knowledgeable** [nɑ́lidʒəbl]	知識豊かな、博識な
27	**casually** [kǽʒuəli]	不用意に

その他

30	**variable** [véəriəbl]	変数

本文解説 & Check Drill

---

1 【関係代名詞の省略】（第 1 段落第 2 文）

Donald Olson, an expert in physics, and a team of scientists have examined the role **(which[that])** the moon may have played in the disaster.

▶ 目的格の関係代名詞 whom, which, that などは省略されることが多い。省略された結果、〈名詞 ＋ Ｓ Ｖ〉の形になることに注意。

▶ 〈前置詞＋関係代名詞〉（in which など）や非制限用法の関係代名詞は省略することができない。

---

2 【enough to 不定詞】（第 3 段落第 7 文）

The high tide caused by the strange combination of events would have been **enough to** separate icebergs ...

▶ 〈enough + to 不定詞〉は、〈too ... to 不定詞〉と同様、程度を表す不定詞の用法の 1 つである。「とても［十分に］～なので…できる」という意味が基本。

▶ enough を含む句の語順は〈形容詞［副詞］＋ enough〉、〈enough ＋ 名詞〉となる。上の文は、enough が単独で用いられている例である。また、不定詞の意味上の主語は for で表す。

---

3 【不定詞の副詞的用法：be hard to *do*】（第 5 段落第 1 文）

The probability of all these variables lining up in just the way they did was, well, **hard to imagine**.

▶ 不定詞の副詞的用法には、「目的・結果・感情の理由・判断の根拠」などのほかに、直前の形容詞の意味を限定する用法がある。文の主語が、不定詞の意味上の目的語になっている点に注意。これは形式主語を用いた構文に書き換えることができる。

ex. My E-mail address is **easy to remember**. = It is easy to remember my E-mail address.
　　　「私の E メールのアドレスは覚えやすい」

Check Drill　1～3 は語句を並べ替え、4、5 は間違っている箇所を指摘し、正しい形に直すか、不要と答えよ。

1. 子どもが読めるようなやさしい本は持っていません。　　　　　　　　　　　　　　　　　　　　　（東洋大）

I don't have any books (are / children / to / read / that / for / easy).

2. この家は私たちが住めるだけの広さがある。　　　　　　　　　　　　　　　　　　　　　　　　（東洋大）

This house is (enough / for / in / large / us / live / to).

3. The company (six years / my father / for / ago / worked) does not exist now.　　　　（法政大）

4. ①Kindergarten is a school for children not ②enough old ③to go to ④elementary school.　（会津大）

5. ①The female ②mentality is difficult to ③understand ④it.　　　　　　　　　　　　　　　（上智大）

展開	段落	要旨
導入	1	タイタニック号は氷山に衝突し沈没した。科学者たちはなぜ（①　　　　　　　　　　　　　）が氷山の警告に注意を払わなかったのかを研究してきた。
本論①	2	（②　　　　　）の異常接近により潮位が上昇し、通常より多くの氷山が（③　　　　　　　　）から分離したことが、氷山が航路まで達する原因となった可能性がある。
本論②	3	沈没の3か月前、非常に珍しい出来事が偶然重なった。これにより、（②　　　　　）の潮汐力が最大になり、分離した氷山は3か月間浮遊し航路に到達した。
本論③	4	その研究は、氷山に対する（①　　　　　　　　　　　）の対応には責任を負わせられないかもしれないということを示している。
結論	5	（①　　　　　　　　　　　）が、このような事態が起こることを（④　　　　　　）することは難しかっただろう。

■　以下を参考にして、「段落要旨」の下線部分を中心にまとめてみよう。
　▶「導入」と「本論①」の内容（70〜80字）
　【記述例】：「〜の原因は…だった可能性がある」
　・「結論」の内容（15〜25字）

（下書き）

									10										20

									10										20

In junior high school, one of my classmates had a TV addiction* — back before ⬦43
it was normal. This boy — we'll call him Ethan — watched TV all day long and
knew almost everything about TV comic shows.

Then one day, Ethan's mother made him (1)a bold offer. If he could go a full
month without watching any TV, she would give him $200. None of us thought he
could do it. But Ethan quit TV quite easily. His friends offered to let him (2)cheat
at their houses on Friday nights. Ethan said no. One month later, Ethan's mom paid
him $200. He went out and bought a TV, the biggest one he could find.

Since there have been children, there have been adults trying to get them to obey ⬦44
their parents. The Bible repeatedly commands children to listen to their parents and
proposes that disobedient* children be killed by throwing stones at them, or at least
have their eyes picked out by cruel birds. Over the centuries, (3)the stick has lost favor
to the carrot in most cases. Today adults start rewarding kids with cheap gifts, such
as a candy for using the toilet or a cookie for sitting still in church, before kids can
speak in full sentences.

In recent years, hundreds of schools in the USA have made these transactions ⬦45
more businesslike, experimenting with paying kids with real money for showing up
in class, getting good grades or going another day without fighting.

I have not met a child who does not admire this trend. But (4)it makes adults ⬦46
terribly uncomfortable. Teachers complain that we are rewarding kids for doing what
they should be doing of their own will. Psychologists warn that money can actually
make kids perform worse, because it makes them lose respect for the act of learning.
Parents predict that kids will be lazy after the incentives go away. (5)The debate has
become a big battle that caused the larger dispute over why our kids are not learning at
the rate they should be despite decades of reforms and budget increases.

But all this time, there has been only one real question, particularly in America's ⬦47
lowest-performing schools: Does it work?

   * addiction「中毒」 disobedient「言うことをきかない」

❶ ....

❷ ....

❸ ....

❹ ....

....

❺ ....

....

❻ ....

❼ ....

語句　音声は、「英語」→「日本語の意味」の順で読まれます。　　　　CD 2 - Tr 48 〜 51

入試基本レベル	
2	**normal** [nɔ́:rməl]（形）
6	**quit** [kwít]
11	**propose** [prəpóuz]
12	**favor** [féivər]（名）
13	**reward** [riwɔ́:rd]（動）
17	**experiment with ~**
17	**show up**
19	**trend** [trénd]
20	**terribly** [térəbli]
20	**complain** [kəmpléin]
21	**warn** [wɔ́:rn]
22	**respect** [rispékt]（名）
23	**lazy** [léizi]
25	**despite** [dispáit]

10	**command** [kəmǽnd]（動）
12	**cruel** [krú:əl]
19	**admire** [ədmáiər]
21	**psychologist** [saikálədʒist]
23	**predict** [pridíkt]
23	**debate** [dibéit]（名）
25	**decade** [dékeid]
25	**reform** [rifɔ́:rm]（名）

入試発展レベル（二次・有名私大）	
4	**bold** [bóuld]	大胆な
16	**transaction** [trænsǽkʃən]	取引
24	**dispute** [dispjú:t]（名）	論争
25	**budget** [bʌ́dʒət]	予算

入試標準レベル（共通テスト・私大）	
6	**cheat** [tʃí:t]（動）
9	**obey** [oubéi]
10	**repeatedly** [ripí:tidli]

その他	
21	**of *one's* own will**	自分の意志で
23	**incentive** [inséntiv]（名）	奨励金

本文解説 & Check Drill

1 【let ＋ O ＋原形不定詞】(第 2 段落第 5 文)

His friends offered to **let** him cheat at their houses on Friday nights.

▶ let は、make 同様、第 5 文型の動詞として〈let ＋ O ＋原形不定詞〉の形をとり、「O に～させる」という使役の意味を表す。make は「強制的に～させる」という意味を伴うが、let は「～することを許可する、～させてあげる」を表す。

2 【get ＋ O ＋ to 不定詞】(第 3 段落第 1 文)

Since there have been children, there have been adults trying to **get** them to obey their parents.

▶ get にも使役動詞としての用法があるが、目的補語には原形不定詞ではなく to 不定詞を用いる。〈get ＋ O ＋ to 不定詞〉の形を取る。
▶ O と C の関係が「受動」の場合、to 不定詞に代わって過去分詞が用いられる。
　ex. Be sure to **get** it **done** by tomorrow.
　（必ず明日までにそれを仕上げてください）

3 【仮定法現在】(第 3 段落第 2 文)

The Bible repeatedly commands children to listen to their parents and **proposes** that disobedient children **be killed** by throwing stones at them …

▶「命令・提案・要求」などを表す動詞が目的語に that 節が用いられる場合、that 節の中の動詞は原形が用いられる。この動詞の原形を「仮定法現在」と呼ぶ。
▶ イギリス英語では、that 節の中の動詞が〈should ＋原形〉になることもある。

Check Drill 　1、2 は語句を並べ替え、3 ～ 5 は空所に適切なものを入れなさい。

1. 飛行機に乗り遅れないように、わたしはタクシーの運転手に急いでもらった。　　　　　(東京工科大)
   I (the taxi driver / so / to hurry / got / as) not to miss my plane.

   ....

2. 町長は、大学のそばに新しい診療所を建ててはどうかと提案した。　　　　　(中央大)
   The town's (new / that / be / mayor / a / suggested / built / clinic) near the university.

   ....

3. She never (　　　) her son play outside unless she was watching.　　　　　(桜花学園大)
   ① permitted　　　② let　　　③ got　　　④ allowed

4. Mr. White (　　　) his daughter to attend the ceremony in his place.　　　　　(大阪医科大)
   ① got　　　② made　　　③ let　　　④ talked

5. The workers demanded that the company (　　　) overtime.　　　　　(上智大)
   ① will pay　　　② pay　　　③ paid　　　④ had paid

展開	段落	要旨
導入①	1	私が中学生の頃、（① 　　　　　　　　）中毒のクラスメートがいた。
導入②	2	彼の母親は彼に、1か月間（① 　　　　　　　　）を見ずに過ごしたら彼に（② 　　　）ドルをあげると約束した。1か月後、彼は（② 　　　　）ドルを得て大きな（① 　　　　　　　）を買った。
本論①	3	親は様々な方法で子どもに言うことを聞かせようとする。最近では、多くの親はしつけのために、罰を与えるのではなく（③ 　　　　　　）を与えている。
本論②	4	アメリカの学校が、模範的な行動をした生徒に（④ 　　　　　　）を与える実験を行った。
本論③	5	教育現場に（③ 　　　　　　　）を与えることが持ち込まれると、子どもが自分の意志で学ぶ欲求を失うのではという懸念がある。それらを巡る議論は、教育現場で行われてきた様々な努力にも関わらず、子どもたちが適切な進度で学べていないのはなぜか、というより大きな論争を引き起こしている。
結び	6	しかし、本当の疑問は、それは「（⑤ 　　　　　　　　　　　）」ということである。

■　以下を参考にして、「段落要旨」の下線部分を中心にまとめてみよう。
　▶「本論①」の内容（25〜35字）
　▶「本論③」の内容（65〜75字）
　【記述例】：「学校にそれが持ち込まれると、〜ではと懸念されている」
　【言い換え例】：「適切な進度で学べていない」→「学力低迷（状態）」

（下書き）

The number of road deaths in Japan in 2018 was a record low of 3,532. The
National Police Agency reported that this reduction since the peak in 1970 of over
16,000 was due to more traffic safety education. The introduction of seat belts, air
bags and other safety equipment into cars since 1970 is also likely to be a factor.
5 Three thousand five hundred is still a high number, averaging roughly ten per day.
Many people dream that self-driving cars (SDC) will greatly increase road safety. To
date, the accidents involving SDCs have been caused by humans. The hope is that
when all cars are SDCs, human error will be (A)eradicated, and road deaths become
a thing of the past.

10 However pleasant this idea may be, it remains a dream. SDCs need to be
programmed to predict as many situations as possible to reduce danger. Certainly,
unexpected situations will still occur, such as people breaking the law at red lights
and walking into the oncoming traffic. A major question arises; when danger cannot
be circumvented, how should SDCs be programmed to respond?

15 The English philosopher Phillipa Foot introduced a thought experiment called
the *Trolley Problem*. A driverless train is going along a track which divides into two
branches. On one branch, five people are tied up on the track. On the other branch,
one person is tied up. The train cannot be stopped, and it will hit the five people. A
switch controls which branch the train travels. You have (1)two options: 1) to press
20 the switch to move the train onto the other track. This means that one person will
be hit, but that you will have initiated this; 2) to do nothing. In this case, five people
will be hit, but you will not be involved in the accident. In tests, most people *say* that
they will press the switch and save five lives.

The Trolley Problem is useful for future SDC technology because it gets people
25 to think about issues that are important in road safety. Should SDCs be programmed
to, for example, save more or fewer lives? The options can be changed to other
choices. Should young people's lives be saved instead of old people's? Females or
males? Doctors or homeless people? Healthy or unhealthy? The list goes on. A
team of scientists from the Massachusetts Institute of Technology (MIT) created a
30 website to ask these questions. By 2018, the MIT team had collected over 40 million
responses from all over the world. The results were (B)intriguing: females are more
important than males; younger people more valuable than older people; high-status
citizens more meaningful than low-status individuals. Differences between cultures
were also observed. For example, Eastern countries, including Japan, preferred to

(2-1) the (2-2) of lawful people, but Southern countries, such as Brazil, did not. ₃₅

So far, however, these tests are only thought experiments. (3)What people *say* they will do and what they *actually* do may be very different. What we say is based on how we *think*. But are we *really* the people we think we are? In 2018, an American TV show *Mind Field* tested this question with real people. Making this show was very dangerous in terms of morals because it can cause severe psychological damage to ₄₀ the people in the study. The information learned from the show, however, indicated that many people would be paralyzed; they could do nothing. The message for SDCs is highly complex. From now on, there needs to be a serious discussion between governments, car manufacturers and consumer groups about how SDCs should respond to unusual situations. (4)This is likely to be an intriguing and extremely ₄₅ valuable discussion.

1 (A) .... (B) ....

2 ....

3 (2-1) .... (2-2) ....

4 ....

5 ....
....

6 ....

語句　音声は、「英語」→「日本語の意味」の順で読まれます。　　CD 2 - Tr 57 〜 60

入試基本レベル

4	**equipment** [ikwípmənt]	
4	**factor** [fǽktər]	
5	**average** [ǽvəridʒ] （動）	
14	**respond** [rispánd]	
16	**track** [trǽk]	
17	**branch** [brǽntʃ]	（鉄道の）支線
17	*be* **tied up**	
19	**control** [kəntróul]	
25	**issue** [íʃuː]	
27	**instead of** 〜	
31	**response** [rispáns]	
37	*be* **based on** 〜	
40	**severe** [sivíər]	
44	**manufacturer** [mæ̀njəfǽktʃərər]	

入試標準レベル（共通テスト・私大）

2	**reduction** [ridʌ́kʃən]	
2	**peak** [píːk]	
5	**roughly** [rʌ́fli]	
7	**involve** [inválv]	
11	**predict** [pridíkt]	
12	**unexpected** [ʌ̀nikspéktəd]	
15	**philosopher** [filásəfər]	
16	**divide into** 〜	
40	**in terms of** 〜	
40	**psychological** [sàikəládʒikəl]	
41	**indicate** [índikèit]	
43	**complex** [kɑmpléks]	
45	**extremely** [ikstríːmli]	

入試発展レベル（二次・有名私大）

6	**self-driving car**	自動運転車
13	**arise** [əráiz]	発生する
31	**intriguing** [intríːgiŋ]	興味をそそる、非常に面白い
35	**lawful** [lɔ́ːfəl]	法を順守する

その他

1	**road death**	交通事故死（者）
1	**the National Police Agency**	警察庁
8	**eradicate** [irǽdikèit]	〜を撲滅する
13	**oncoming** [ánkʌ̀miŋ] （形）	近づいてくる
14	**circumvent** [sə̀ːrkəmvént]	〜を回避する
15	**thought experiment**	思考実験
16	**trolley** [tráli]	路面電車、トロリーバス
16	**driverless** [dráivərləs]	運転手のいない
21	**initiate** [iníʃièit]	〜を開始する
29	**the Massachusetts Institute of Technology (MIT)**	マサチューセッツ工科大学
32	**high-status**	高い地位の
33	**low-status**	低い地位の
42	**paralyzed** [pǽrəlàizd]	麻痺（まひ）した

1 【複合関係詞 however】（第 2 段落第 1 文）

However pleasant this idea may be, it remains a dream.

▶ 関係詞に -ever をつけた語を複合関係詞と呼び、複合関係代名詞と複合関係副詞とがある。複合関係代名詞 whoever, whichever, whatever は名詞節あるいは副詞節を導く。複合関係副詞 wherever, whenever, however は副詞節を導く。

▶ however は多くの場合〈however ＋形容詞［副詞］＋ SV ...〉の形で用いられ、「たとえどんなに～であっても」という「譲歩」の意味を表す。上記の文は「この考えがどんなに魅力的なものであっても、それはまだ夢のままだ」の意味。

▶ however が導く節の中には、上記の例のように助動詞 may を伴うものもある。また、however ～ を no matter how ～ と書き換えることもできる。

2 【複雑な関係詞の文 ― 関係詞の直後に〈主語＋動詞〉が挿入される場合】（第 5 段落第 2、4 文）

A. **What people *say* they will do** and what they *actually* do may be very different.

▶ 関係代名詞 what の直後に〈主語＋動詞〉が挿入されている。what (people *say*) they will do のように people say をいったん（　　）に入れるとわかりやすい。what は say の目的語ではなく、do の目的語の働きをしていて、「人々が、自分たちがやると『言う』こと」の意味。

▶ この用法は what だけでなく、先行詞がある関係代名詞 who, which, that でも用いられる。また、関係代名詞の直後に使われる動詞には think, believe, know, hear, suppose などがある。

B. But are we *really* **the people we think we are**?

▶ we think we are は the people を先行詞とする関係代名詞節で、the people (that) we think we are の that が省略されている。これも、関係代名詞の直後に we think という〈主語＋動詞〉が挿入されている。関係代名詞 that は are の補語になっていて、「私たちが、自分たちはそうだと考えているような人間」の意味。

▶ be 動詞の補語として働く関係代名詞は that が好まれるが、この例のように省かれることも多い。

Check Drill　1 ～ 3 は空所に入る適切なものを選び、4、5 は語句を並べ替えなさい。

1. (　　　　), you must finish the work today.

① However tired you may be　　② However you may be tired
③ However tired are you　　④ However are you tired　　（県立広島大）

2. The man (　　) I believed was one of the executives turned out to be a part-time worker.

① what　　② which　　③ who　　④ whose　　（日本大）

3. He is not (　　) we think him to be.

① what　　② who　　③ that　　④ how　　（京都薬科大・改）

4. どんなに強くそのドアを押しても、どうしても開かなかった。　　（國學院大）

(pushed / hard / however / the door / I), it wouldn't open.

5. 正しいと思うことをするには時に勇気がいる。　　（東海大）

It sometimes takes courage to (is / do / right / you / what / think).

段落要旨　各段落のまとめとなるように、空所に適切な語句を入れなさい。（同じ番号には、同じ語句が入ります）

展開	段落	要旨
導入①	1	交通事故死者数は減少してきたが、その数は依然として多い。今後は（①　　　　　　　　）が人的ミスを撲滅し、交通安全を向上させると期待されている。
導入②	2	しかし、予期しないような状況が起き、危険が避けられない場合、（①　　　　　　　）はどう対応するようにプログラムされるべきだろうか。
本論①	3	（②　　　　　）の命を救うために自ら選択して（③　　　　　）の命を犠牲にするかどうかを問われる、『トロッコ問題』という思考実験がある。この実験では、多くの人が（③　　　　　）の命を犠牲にして（②　　　　　）の命を救う方を選択すると答えた。
本論②	4	『トロッコ問題』は交通安全上の重要問題について考えさせるので、（①　　　　　　　）の技術開発に役立つだろう。どちらの命を救うかを問うMITの調査では、（④　　　　　）や年齢、地位により価値づけに差があることがわかった。また、文化間での回答の違いも見られた。
結論	5	こうした実験は思考実験にすぎず、また人の言葉と（⑤　　　　　）は同じではない。実際に現場で選択を迫るテレビ番組の実験では、誰も何もできなかった。今後、政府、自動車メーカー、消費者団体は（①　　　　　　　）の異常事態への対応について真剣に話し合う必要があり、それは価値ある議論となるだろう。

百字要約　「段落要旨」を参考にして、本文全体の内容を百字程度の日本語で要約しなさい。

■ 以下を参考にして、「段落要旨」の下線部分を中心にまとめてみよう。
▶「導入①、②」の内容（20〜30字）【記述例】：「自動運転車は〜」
▶「本論①、②」の内容（30〜40字）
▶「結論」の内容（20〜30字）【記述例】：「異常事態への対応について…」

（下書き）

Memo

We often worry about lying awake in the middle of the night — but it may not be a problem. A growing body of evidence from both science and history suggests that a long and uninterrupted sleep may not be natural.

In the early 1990s, researcher Thomas Wehr conducted (1)an experiment in which a group of people were kept in darkness for 14 hours every day for a month. It took some time for their sleep to become regular, but by the fourth week the subjects had settled into a very distinct sleeping pattern. They slept first for four hours, then woke for one or two hours before falling into a second four-hour sleep.

(2)Though sleep scientists paid attention to the results of the study, the idea that we must sleep for eight continuous hours persists among the general public. More recently, in 2001, historian Roger Ekirch of Virginia Tech published an influential paper, drawn from 16 years of research, revealing a lot of historical evidence that humans used to sleep in two distinct periods. His book *At Day's Close: Night in Times Past*, published four years later, presents more than 500 references to (3)a split sleeping pattern — in diaries, court records, medical books, and literature, from ancient Greece to modern Africa.

Much like the experience of Wehr's subjects, these references describe a first sleep which began about two hours after sunset, followed by a waking period of one or two hours and then a second sleep. "It's not just the number of references to this sleeping pattern that is significant, but it's also the way they refer to it, as if it were common knowledge," Ekirch says.

During this waking period, people did all kinds of things. They often got up, went to the toilet or smoked tobacco and some even visited neighbors. People read, wrote, and often prayed. Countless prayer manuals from the late 15th century offered special prayers for the hours in between sleeps. Ekirch found that references to the first and second sleep began to disappear during the late 17th century. (4)This started among the urban upper classes in northern Europe, and over the course of the next 200 years gradually influenced the rest of Western society. By the 1920s, the idea of a first and second sleep had disappeared completely.

Ekirch gives the reasons for the initial shift as improvements in street lighting, home lighting and an increase in coffee houses, which were sometimes open all night. (5)As the night became a time for increased activity, the length of time people could spend resting decreased. With the introduction of street lighting, socializing at night slowly became common among all social classes. In 1667, Paris became the first city in the world to light its streets, using wax candles in glass lamps. It was followed by Amsterdam two years later, where a much more efficient oil-powered lamp was developed. London did not install street lighting until 1684, but by the end of the century, more than 50 of Europe's major towns and cities were lit at night. Nighttime activities became fashionable, so people went to bed later, and (6   ).

1

2

3
4

5

6
7

語句　音声は、「英語」→「日本語の意味」の順で読まれます。　CD 2 - Tr 67～70

入試基本レベル

2	suggest [sʌgdʒést]	
8	fall into sleep	
13	period [píəriəd]	
15	medical [médikəl]	
15	literature [lítərətʃər]	
15	ancient [éinʃənt]	
17	describe [diskráib]	
20	refer to ～	
23	neighbor [néibər]（名）	
24	offer [ɔ́(:)fər]（動）	
26	disappear [dìsəpíər]	
28	gradually [grǽdʒuəli]	
28	influence [ínfluəns]（動）	
30	improvement [imprúːvmənt]	
31	increase [ínkriːs]（名）	
33	decrease [dìːkríːs]（動）	
39	fashionable [fǽʃənəbl]	

入試標準レベル （共通テスト・私大）

2	evidence [évid(e)ns]	
4	conduct [kəndʌ́kt]（動）	
6	subject [sʌ́bdʒekt]（名）	
7	settle [sétl]	
7	distinct [distíŋkt]	
9	pay attention to ～	
10	continuous [kəntínjuəs]	
10	general public	
11	influential [influénʃəl]	
12	reveal [rivíːl]（動）	
14	present [prizént]（動）	
14	reference [réfərəns]（名）	
14	split [splít]（形）	
15	court [kɔ́ːrt]（名）	
20	significant [signífikənt]	
24	manual [mǽnjuəl]（名）	
27	urban [ə́ːrbn]	
27	course [kɔ́ːrs]（名）	
28	rest [rést]（名）	
30	initial [iníʃəl]	

30	shift [ʃíft]（名）	
36	efficient [ifíʃənt]	

入試発展レベル （二次・有名私大）

3	uninterrupted [ʌ̀nintərʌ́ptid]	間断ない
10	persist [pərsíst]	残る、持続する
24	pray [préi]	祈る
24	countless [káuntləs]	数えきれない、無数の
24	prayer [préər]	祈り
27	upper class	上流階級
37	install [instɔ́ːl]	～を設置する、取り付ける

その他

2	a body of ～	一連の～、大量の～
33	socialize [sóuʃəlàiz]	社交的に活動する
35	wax candle	ろうそく

1 【前置詞＋関係代名詞】(第2段落第1文)

In the early 1990s, researcher Thomas Wehr conducted an experiment **in which** a group of people were kept in darkness for 14 hours every day for a month.

▶ 関係代名詞には、直前に前置詞を伴う用法がある。この文では、which の先行詞は experiment で、in which = in the experiment という関係になる。この用法では、関係代名詞 that は用いられない。

2 【同格表現】(第3段落第1文)

... the idea **that** we must sleep for eight continuous hours persists among the general public.

▶ 接続詞 that には、直前の名詞を説明する「同格」の名詞節を導く用法がある。この文では the idea と that 節の we must sleep for eight continuous hours がイコールの関係になっていて、「～ (that 節の内容) という考え」と訳せばよい。

3 【強調構文】(第4段落第2文)

It's not just the number of references to this sleeping pattern **that** is significant, ...

▶ 〈It is ... that ～〉の ... の部分に強調したい語句 (主に名詞や代名詞、前置詞句、副詞 (句)、副詞節) を入れた文を強調構文という。上の例では、not just the number of references to this sleeping pattern が強調されている。文頭の It は訳さずに、「～ (that 以下) なのは…である」のように訳すと自然な日本語になることが多い。

Check Drill　　1～3は語句を並べ替え、4、5は空所に適切なものを入れて日本語に訳しなさい。

1. あなたがたが住んでいるこの美しい地球を大切にしなければならない。　　　　(愛知工業大)

You must (are / which / this beautiful earth / you / on / take care of) living.

2. 彼女は息子がけがをしたという知らせを聞いて驚いた。　　　　(近畿大)

She was surprised (at / got / her son / injured / that / the news).

3. 昨日彼が目を覚ましたのは正午近くだった。　　　　(明星大・改)

It (at / he / noon / that / was / woke / nearly) up yesterday.

4. The fact (　　　) he came back safely made everyone happy.　　　　(北星学園大・改)

　① how　　　　　② that　　　　　③ what　　　　　④ in which

5. For human beings and all other animals, (　　　) is oxygen that makes life on earth possible.

　① what　　　　② which　　　　③ only　　　　④ it　　　　(酪農学園大)

段落要旨 　各段落のまとめとなるように、空所に適切な語句を入れなさい。（同じ番号には、同じ語句が入ります）

展開	段落	要旨
導入①	1	長い時間（①　　　　　）しない眠りは不自然かもしれない、という証拠がある。
本論①	2	人々を1ヶ月間、暗闇に1日（②　　　　　）時間とどめておく実験が行われた。被験者たちは最初の眠りのあと1、2時間起きていて、その後また眠るようになった。
本論②	3	ある本は、かつて人々が（③　　　　　）に分かれた2つの時間帯に眠っていたことを示す証拠を数多く紹介した。
本論③	4	それらの引用例は、まるで（④　　　　　）であるかのように、分割型の睡眠パターンを描写していた。
本論④	5	人々は2つの眠りの間の時間に様々なことをしていた。しかし、（⑤　　　　　）世紀後半には、2つの眠りに関する言及はなくなり始めた。
本論⑤	6	街灯の進歩や、夜間営業の（⑥　　　　　）の増加によって、睡眠パターンは変化し始めた。夜間の活動が流行した結果、人々の寝る時間は（⑦　　　　　）なり、一続きの睡眠をとるようになったのだ。

百字要約 　「段落要旨」を参考にして、本文全体の内容を百字程度の日本語で要約しなさい。

- ■ 以下を参考にして、「段落要旨」の下線部分を中心にまとめてみよう。
  - ▶「本論①、②」の内容（25〜35字）【記述例】:「実験結果や歴史的証拠によれば、かつて人間は〜だった」
  - ▶「本論③、④」の内容は「本論②」の補足情報のため、ここでは省略。
  - ▶「本論⑤」の内容（65〜75字）【記述例】:「それらが変化した原因は〜であり、夜間活動が流行した結果…」

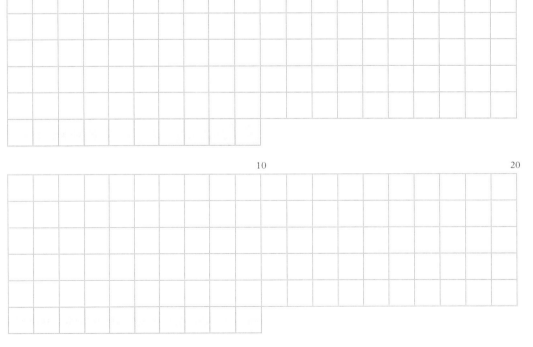

（下書き）

Memo

There is (1)a paradox* at the heart of our lives. Most people want more income and work hard for it. Yet, as Western societies have got richer, their people have become no happier. This is no old wives' tale. It is a fact proven by many pieces of scientific research. As I'll show, we have good ways to measure how happy people are, and all the evidence says that on average people are no happier today than people were fifty years ago. At the same time, however, average incomes have doubled. This paradox is equally true for the United States, Britain and Japan.

But aren't our lives infinitely more comfortable? Indeed: we have more food, more clothes, more cars, more holidays and, above all, better health. Yet we are not happier. Despite all the efforts of governments, teachers and doctors which have improved our lives, human happiness has not increased. Suppose you were asked to choose between living in two imaginary worlds, in which prices were the same. In the first of these worlds you would get $50,000 a year, compared with an average income of $25,000. In the second of these worlds you would get $100,000 a year, compared with an average income of $250,000. Which do you choose? This question was put to a group of Harvard students and (2)the majority preferred the first type of world. They were happy to be poorer, if their relative position improved. People care greatly about their relative income, and they would be willing to accept a significant fall as long as they could improve their position in relation to other people.

People also compare their income with what they themselves are used to. When they are asked how much income they need, richer people always say they need more than poorer people. So (3)whether you are happy with your income depends on how it compares with some standard. And that standard depends on two things: what other people get and what you yourself are accustomed to getting. In the first case your feelings are governed by social comparison, and in the second by your ability to get used to things.

Because these two forces are so strong in human nature, it is quite difficult for economic growth to improve our happiness. The reason for this is that as actual incomes rise, the standard by which income is judged rises in step. You can see this from data collected by the Gallup Poll* in the United States over many years. People were asked, "What is the smallest amount of money a family of four needs to get along reasonably well in this community? " (4)The chart shows how much money people thought they needed to live comfortably — that is, their "required income," and how much money they actually earn — that is, their "actual income." According to the chart, as people's actual income increases, the amount of money they say they need also increases. So even though people become richer, they are never satisfied. They never say, "I earn much more than I need, so I am happy." They simply feel that they need more money to be happy. This explains why people become no happier even when their standard of living improves.

75   These facts are truly depressing, because they mean that (5)we cannot be happier however much money we might get. But at the same time, they teach us a useful lesson: financial success is not always necessary for your happiness, and to find another aspect of life that satisfies you is an easier way of becoming happy.

  * paradox「逆説」 Gallup Poll「ギャラップ調査（世論調査の一種）」

1

2

3

4

5

6

| 語句 | 音声は、「英語」→「日本語の意味」の順で読まれます。 | CD 2 - Tr 76 ～ 79 |

入試基本レベル

1 **income** [ínkʌm] ....

3 **prove** [prúːv] ....

4 **measure** [méʒər] （動） ....

5 **on average** ....

7 *be* **true for** ～ ....

8 **comfortable** [kʌ́mftəbl] ....

10 **despite** [dispáit] ....

10 **effort** [éfərt] ....

11 **improve** [imprúːv] ....

13 **compare A with B** ....

16 **majority** [mədʒɔ́(ː)rəti] ....

16 **prefer** [prifə́ːr] ....

17 **relative** [rélətiv] ....

18 **care about** ～ ....

23 **depend on** ～ ....

24 **standard** [stǽndərd] （名） ....

28 **force** [fɔ́ːrs] （名） ....

32 **get along** ....

35 **according to** ～ ....

入試標準レベル （共通テスト・私大）

5 **evidence** [évidns] ....

8 **indeed** [indíːd] ....

12 **imaginary** [imǽdʒənèri] ....

18 *be* **willing to** *do* ....

19 **significant** [signífikənt] ....

24 **compare with** ～ ....

25 *be* **accustomed to** ～ ....

26 **govern** [gʌ́vərn] ....

26 **comparison** [kəmpǽrisn] ....

34 **required** [rikwáiərd] ....

37 **satisfy** [sǽtisfài] ....

41 **depressing** [diprésiŋ] ....

43 **financial** [fənǽnʃl] ....

43 **aspect** [ǽspekt] ....

入試発展レベル （二次・有名私大）

1 **paradox** [pǽrədàks] 逆説、矛盾

8 **infinitely** [ínfənətli] 無限に、大いに

その他

3 **old wives' tale** 言い伝え、迷信

1 【no more … than 〜】 (第1段落第6文)

…, all the evidence says that on average people are **no happier** today **than** people were fifty years ago.

▶ no more … than 〜は2つの文の否定の度合いが同じであることを示す構文である。「〜が…でないのと同じように、〜も…ではない」と訳す。more … のところに形容詞がくる場合は、上の例のようにhappier という比較級になる。

2 【関係代名詞 what】 (第3段落第1文)

People also compare their income with **what** they themselves are used to.

▶ 関係代名詞 what は先行詞をそれ自身の中に含む関係代名詞で、「〜するもの［こと］」という日本語に対応する。what が導く節は、原則的に名詞節である。上の例は、what 節が前置詞 with の目的語の働きをしている。また、what 自身も名詞なので、節の中で名詞としての働きを持つ。上の例では、前置詞 toの目的語が what である。

3 【複合関係詞】 (第5段落第1文)

… we cannot be happier **however** much money we might get.

▶ who、what などに -ever が加わったものを複合関係詞と呼ぶ。whoever は「誰であっても」、whatever は「何であっても」、however は「どれほど〜であっても」という意味になる。whoever、whatever、whichever には名詞節と副詞節の両方の用法があるが、however、whenever、whereverは常に譲歩の副詞節として働く。また、however はその後に形容詞や副詞を伴う。上の例は howevermuch money がひとまとまりになっている。

Check Drill　1〜3は語句を並べ替え、4、5は空所に適切なものを入れなさい。

1. 私も彼と同じように、この機械を動かすことができない。　　　　(北海道文教大)

   I am (this machine / able / more / operate / than / no / to) he is.

   ....

2. 状況がどんなに困難になろうとも、私たちはそれに立ち向かわなければならない。　(関西学院大)

   (be / difficult / however / out / situation / the / to / turns), we have to confront it.

   ....

3. 私の記憶に一番残っているのは、イギリスで友達と楽しく過ごしたことです。　(桃山学院大)

   (all the fun / I / I had / is / most / remember / what) with my friends in England.

   ....

4. (　　　　) wishes to join the travel must gather in front of the station at 8:00 a.m.　(埼玉医科大)

   ① Anybody　　　　② Everybody　　　　③ Those who　　　　④ Whoever

5. (　　　　) seems easy at first often turns out to be difficult.　(センター試験)

   ① It　　　　② That　　　　③ What　　　　④ Which

段落要旨　各段落のまとめとなるように、空所に適切な語句を入れなさい。（同じ番号には、同じ語句が入ります）

展開	段落	要旨
主題	1	私たちの人生には１つの逆説がある。<u>たとえ私たちが以前より豊かになっても、より</u> （①　　　　　　）<u>にはなっていない</u>ということだ。
本論①	2	ある調査において、人々は（②　　　　　　）な収入を非常に気にするということが明らかになった。
本論②	3	人々は自分の収入に対する満足度を、ある（③　　　　）と比べることで決める。その （③　　　　　　）は、他人の収入と、自分が手にすることに慣れている収入の２つによって決まる。
本論③	4	これが、（④　　　　　　）な成長が私たちの（①　　　　　　）を向上させることは難しい理由 だ。より多くのお金を稼ぎ始めるにつれ、収入を判断する基準も上がる。
結論	5	自分を満足させる人生の（⑤　　　　　　）を発見する方が、（①　　　　　　）になる簡単な 方法である。

百字要約　「段落要旨」を参考にして、本文全体の内容を百字程度の日本語で要約しなさい。

■ 以下を参考にして、「段落要旨」の下線部分を中心にまとめてみよう。
▶「主題」の内容（20〜30字）
▶「本論①、③」の内容（35〜40字）
▶「結論」の内容（30〜40字）

（下書き）　　　　　　　　　　　　　　　　　　10　　　　　　　　　　　　　　　　　　20

Memo

Cutting Edge Green

Navi Book 【付録】

編著者　山本一太

株式会社 エミル出版

〒 102-0072 東京都千代田区飯田橋 2-8-1

【電　　話】03-6272-5481

【ファックス】03-6272-5482

2024.1

Cutting Edge Green
Navi Book

カッティングエッジ・グリーン
ナビブック 〔付録〕

検印欄

1	2	3	4	5	6
7	8	9	10	11	12
13	14	15	16	17	18

年　　　組　　　番　氏名